Uncle Bubba's
Chicken Wing Fling

Mitchel Whitington

Republic of Texas Press
Plano, TX

Library of Congress Cataloging-in-Publication Data

Whitington, Mitchel.
  Uncle Bubba's chicken wing fling / by Mitchel Whitington.
      p.   cm.
  ISBN 1-55622-695-0 (pbk.)
  1. Texas—Humor.   2. Texas—Social life and customs—Humor
  3. Cookery (Chicken).   I. Title.
  PN6231.T56 W48   1999
  641.6'65'00207—dc21   99-026675
                                                              CIP

Republic of Texas Press is an imprint of Wordware Publishing, Inc.
No part of this book may be reproduced in any form or by
any means without permission in writing from
Wordware Publishing, Inc.

Printed in the United States of America

ISBN 1-55622-695-0
10 9 8 7 6 5 4 3 2 1
9911

All inquiries for volume purchases of this book should be addressed to
Wordware Publishing, Inc., at 2320 Los Rios Boulevard, Plano, Texas 75074.
Telephone inquiries may be made by calling:

(972) 423-0090

For Tami,
the Aunt Irma
in the Cut Plug
that is my life.

"Whitington's writing voice is gentle and easy, like water flowing over smooth stones. Uncle Bubba's adventures are down home—funny and refreshing!"

—Denise Vitola, lecturer and author of the Ty Merrick Sci-fi series

"Mr. Whitington wastes no time spinning his story. The details are exquisite, and his sense of characters puts you front and center in a story that tickles your mind, heart, and all your senses. In just a few paragraphs, he placed me right in the middle of Cut Plug. Meeting the townspeople made me feel like an old friend."

—James E. Gardiner, author of the new action-thriller *Capitol Chill*

"After reading the tales of Cut Plug you can almost smell the bar-b-cue sauce and hear the baying of the hunting dogs as they catch the first scent of Uncle Bubba's wings. Good-hearted Uncle Bubba has that lovable knack for getting himself into the thick of it and tickling our funny-bone along the way."

—Ronald Wayne Jones, author of *The Dwarf and the Demon Tongue*

Table of Contents

The First Things My Uncle Taught Me

Every small town in Texas is full of characters, and Cut Plug is certainly no different. I could tell stories about our little community all day long.

To be honest, though, there is no single Cut Plug citizen that raises more eyebrows and makes more waves than my Uncle Bubba.

Uncle Bubba has been a huge presence in my life since the day I was born, and I'm proud of that fellow. In spite of all the trouble that people have attributed to him over the years, his heart of gold always shines through.

My uncle has his talents, too, not the least of which is cooking chicken wings. When it comes to that one particular subject, the man is a regular Michelangelo. People in Cut Plug are always looking for a chance to try one of his exotic batches of wings.

Now it's a known fact that Pastor Frawley drives through town every Sunday after church, looking for wisps of smoke behind people's houses—a sure sign that a grill has been fired up for lunch. Occasionally he'll have bad luck, like that one day last fall when all he could find were people out burning leaves. But when he did locate a meal in progress, he'd struck gold— it's impossible not to invite the local preacher to stay for lunch, of course.

Uncle Bubba ended up feeding Pastor Frawley and his wife every few weeks or so, which of course was just fine with Aunt Irma. My uncle didn't mind, either, since the good pastor helped spread the word of how delicious an Uncle Bubba chicken wing really was.

They were quite the couple, my aunt and uncle. He was a big ol' Texas fellow, with a gut that hung over his belt buckle and a perpetual pair of western boots and a gimmie cap. Aunt Irma, on the other hand, was a slight little wisp of a woman. Still, there wasn't any question that she wielded a lot of power—not just with Uncle Bubba, but also with the other organizations that she belonged to. The Book of Ruth Bible class from church and the Cut Plug Garden Club didn't make a single move without her.

It was my Uncle Bubba who always looked after me, though. I'd like to tell you that the first things my uncle taught me in life were about world peace, high finance, and complex mathematical equations. To be truthful, though, the first words of instruction that I remember receiving from my uncle were about cooking chicken wings.

There are a few great chicken wing truths. Before I get started on the stories about Uncle Bubba and the year that he decided to open a chicken wing restaurant, it would probably be prudent for me to make note of them.

The first involves what a chicken wing actually is. There are three pieces to the whole wing: the drumette, the wing piece, and the tip. These are fairly evident when raw wings are purchased at the grocery store. In Cut Plug, we buy these by the dozen at the meat counter over at Hinkley's Grocery. With any respectable wing recipe, you begin by dividing each chicken wing. The drumette portion is pretty obvious—it looks like a small drumstick and is easy to separate from the other pieces. The wing piece is in the middle, and has to be cut away from the tip at the joint. There's no mistaking the tip, since is has no meat at all. It should be discarded. Occasionally I'll see a package of drumettes by themselves at the grocer, and that can save the few minutes it takes to separate the individual pieces. Whether he's referring to the drumette or wing piece, Uncle Bubba makes no distinction—he calls either one a chicken wing. Following my uncle's logic and terminology, to make a twenty-wing recipe you really need only ten of the actual chicken wings, since each one separates into two edible pieces.

The second thing to understand is that while the actual preparation of the wings varies from recipe to recipe, the cooking basically falls into two categories: baking and grilling. The only difference comes down to individual preference, and most recipes are interchangeable when you're trying to determine how to cook them. If I wanted to fix up a batch of Uncle Bubba's wings of one type or another, then the only other decision is whether to fire up the grill or heat up the oven.

That's not to say that many recipes don't have their individual nuances, because they do, and I've pointed them out when necessary. If it's raining outside, though, and I want to fix up a batch of wings that my uncle normally does on the grill, I don't bat an eye at moving them indoors to the oven. Deep-frying is also an option, but for other recipes it just doesn't work out well. For others, though, it's a necessity. Those recipes are best prepared as they were given by my uncle.

Uncle Bubba would almost never fix only one type of chicken wings at a time. He'd usually whip up a couple of flavors, just for variety if nothing else, using the same cooking process for all.

When wings are being prepared in the oven, they're always baked on a greased cookie sheet. This is basically a pan with walls that are only about a half-inch high; this keeps any of those succulent juices from flowing onto the bottom of the oven.

Aunt Irma has also influenced the cooking of chicken wings at their house. She was the first one in town to start using olive oil, since it is the healthiest one on the grocery shelf at the moment. People are always coming up with something new, though, so she's constantly checking the shelves to see what's best.

The other thing that Aunt Irma always insists on is that Uncle Bubba trims as much skin off the wings as possible. This has been a long-standing war in their house and has gained more local notoriety in Cut Plug than the Hatfield/McCoy feud, the constant fussing between the Democrats and the Republicans, or even any of the international conflicts. Aunt Irma wants the skin off for lower fat, but Uncle Bubba wants to leave it on for taste.

Throughout the history of Cut Plug, no year has been more wrought with mischief, calamity, and humor than the year my Uncle Bubba first got it in his head that he wanted to quit his job at the cement plant to open a chicken wing restaurant. I don't think that a single person in Cut Plug was the same after that. I know I certainly wasn't.

Moon Over the Azaleas

Uncle Bubba was dead. At least, I figured that he would be as soon as Aunt Irma caught up with him.

Not that my uncle was really to blame. The whole thing came about through a series of harmless, if not ill timed, events. It was just plain bad luck that put them all together into what Aunt Irma has since referred to as the "Moon Over the Azaleas" incident.

All I knew at the beginning of that Saturday was that Aunt Irma was going to be gone all afternoon, and Uncle Bubba had asked me to come over for some special wings. I knew what this meant, of course—a trip to the county line.

Aunt Irma didn't allow any hard liquor in the house at all— not a single drop. Uncle Bubba always kept a bottle of good Kentucky bourbon out in the garage, and if he wanted to do anything other than sneak out for a few sips with Skeeter and the fellows, he had to wait until Aunt Irma was going to be away.

I drove over to Uncle Bubba's house about midday that Saturday, expecting to see him firing up the grill out back. Instead, Bubba was stomping around the living room, cussing and ranting and spitting out the window every time he walked by.

I couldn't make anything out of what he was saying, so I just took a seat in the recliner and waited for him to calm down. It took a good twenty minutes.

When Uncle Bubba finally stopped and took a deep breath, I knew I was finally going to hear all about it. He grabbed the keys to his truck and motioned toward the door.

He drove toward the interstate and straight to the liquor store. Cut Plug is in a dry precinct, so it was a thirty-minute round trip just to pick up a bottle.

We were halfway to the county line before he finally began to open up a little. It seemed that my uncle had finally taken a step toward realizing his dream: opening a chicken wing restaurant out by the highway. He had apparently got up the nerve to go and talk to the local banker, Mr. Trickle, about a loan to get him started.

One important thing to note about the Cut Plug economy was that it revolves completely around the cement plant at the edge of town. Of the eight hundred people living in Cut Plug, about eighty percent of the adults work there. I guess Mr. Trickle didn't believe in Uncle Bubba's idea enough to give him the money. I sort of understood. Most of the townsfolk brown-bagged it to the plant, and money was always tight enough that eating out was a luxury. Still, my uncle believed in the idea, and he saw it as the only hope he had of getting out of the plant and working for himself.

When we got to the store, Uncle Bubba ran in and got a bottle of Amaretto liqueur. He had to fret over it a little on the way back, saying how he thought it was kind of a sissy drink, but I knew it was just part of the act that he had to go through. A bourbon man had to carry on a bit when purchasing syrupy stuff like that.

I thought he might have been through ranting about banker Trickle, but it wasn't long before he picked right up where he left off. Bubba carried on all the way back to the house and even when he started cooking the wings. He mixed the sauce up on the stove as the wings were baking, all the while giving me the details about the conversation at the bank.

Apparently banker Trickle had offered that Uncle Bubba should just be thankful for the job he had at the plant. Bubba responded by suggesting that Trickle had gotten used to such a cushy job at the bank that he wouldn't be able to survive a single day at the cement plant. From what I understood, things just went downhill from there.

After the sauce was mixed up, Bubba split the remaining Amaretto into two mason jars and we stood around the stove and sipped on it while the wings were baking. This went on for almost an hour, and by the time the wings were ready, Uncle Bubba had a different scheme. He decided that the only way to reclaim his dignity after the incident at the bank was for us to drive over to Mr. Trickle's house, honk the horn, and moon him good when he looked out of the window.

The bank closed at noon since it was Saturday, so I knew Trickle would be home by then, but the whole thing just didn't seem like a well-conceived plan. Uncle Bubba was adamant, though, so I figured if I went along with him, I could steer him away from as much trouble as possible.

I insisted on driving, since I'd only sipped out of my jar and Uncle Bubba had pretty much finished his. We drove three streets over to Mr. Trickle's house, pulled up in the driveway, and I punched the horn a couple of times. The curtains rustled in the front window, and Uncle Bubba quickly dropped his jeans and pressed his rear end up against the glass of the truck's passenger door. Right about that time, Aunt Irma and the rest of the women in the Cut Plug Garden Club walked around the side of the house. They were all decked out in their finest dresses, wearing their hair piled high on their heads, and even sporting spring corsages.

I later found out they were on their Spring Blossom Tour and had stopped at Marianne Trickle's house to see her azalea bushes in full bloom. What they saw, however, was Uncle Bubba's butt cheeks pressed flat against the glass like two giant slugs on the aquarium wall. Time just stopped for a few moments, as the ladies stood there, frozen in horror. Aunt Irma's eyes got wider when she recognized the truck, then her mouth dropped open, and half a minute later she just fainted face-first right over into the azaleas.

Bubba decided that it would be a capital time to spend the rest of the weekend fishing, and last I heard, Aunt Irma was scouring every pond and stream in the county trying to find him.

I stopped back by their house and took the Amaretto wings home with me, of course. There's no need to waste something that tasty. If you'd like to try them for yourself, the recipe is easy.

Amaretto Wings

20 chicken wings
3 Tbsp flour
2 tsp paprika
1 tsp ground white pepper
1 tsp salt
1 tsp dried minced garlic
1 dash red pepper
3 Tbsp vegetable oil
1 cup Amaretto liqueur
1 Tbsp Dijon mustard
1 6¼-oz can frozen concentrated orange juice

Start by preheating your oven to 375 degrees. Mix the flour and dry spices together, then use it to coat the wings. Heat the oil in a skillet, and sauté the wings until they just start to turn brown—do not overcook! Depending on the size of your skillet, this may have to be done in multiple passes. If this is the case, an extra splash of oil may be required. Take the wings out and put them in a casserole dish.

Blend the frozen concentrated orange juice with one-half can of water. Pour it into the skillet, return it to the burner, then add the mustard and Amaretto. Allow the mixture to come to a boil—be sure to stir it continuously. It will eventually thicken. When it does, pour the sauce over the chicken wings. Cover the casserole dish with foil and bake for about 20 minutes or until they're done. By the way, any remaining Amaretto that you didn't use for cooking tastes best just like Uncle Bubba serves it—right out of mason jars.

Uncle Bubba's Easter Angel

Uncle Bubba laid pretty low for a while, just like he did every time he got on the riled side of Aunt Irma. To soothe things over even more, he volunteered to sing in the choir for the Easter cantata.

That tickled Aunt Irma and made up for a multitude of sins. The choir at the Cut Plug Missionary Baptist Church only had eight people on a good Sunday, mostly made up from the church's Book of Ruth Bible class, and Aunt Irma was one of the faithful. The fact that Uncle Bubba was going to participate not only meant that the choir loft would look a little more populated, but they would have a baritone voice for the Easter Angel solo.

Not to say that Uncle Bubba was that accomplished a vocalist. His voice was famous countywide for the hog yell he did whenever he bagged one of those wild pigs during hunting season, but that didn't necessarily translate well to civilized music. Still, he started going to choir practice every single week, getting ready for the big special. I believe he even lost focus on his chicken wing restaurant for a while, because every time I talked to him he was going on about how the choir's musical numbers were coming along, how Mrs. Fenton was doing with her solo, or what he was planning to bring to the covered dish luncheon afterward. A week before Easter he was even speculating about how hard it would be to paint a few pieces of plywood with an Easter background for the choir's special.

This gave me more than a little bit of concern, because I've seen Uncle Bubba like this before. He latches onto a project and throws himself into it with the absolute best of intentions. Somewhere along the way, though, enthusiasm seems to override common sense.

I drove over to their house on Wednesday before choir practice just to check things out for myself. Aunt Irma was still getting ready to leave; she's one of those people who puts on one of her Sunday dresses every time something is happening at the church. She hollered out through the front door that Uncle Bubba was in the garage, so I walked around the house to see what he was up to.

Sure enough, I found Uncle Bubba standing there in his white painting coveralls, spraying a coat of gray paint onto a giant plywood cutout of the biblical tomb, complete with the huge stone rolled to one side. He glanced over his shoulder and said, "Nephew, this is going to be one Easter the congregation will remember forever!"

Yep, I could see that look in his eye. I offered to help, hoping I could be the voice of reason in this endeavor, but he assured me that he and Skeeter had everything under control.

Skeeter was Uncle Bubba's best friend in the whole world. They'd known each other since grade school, and he stood as best man at Bubba and Irma's wedding.

Everyone who knows Bubba is aware that he cuts a pretty big profile, especially around the belly. As chunky as Uncle Bubba is, though, Skeeter is just as skinny. That wispy fellow looks even thinner when they're standing next to each other, so I guess they complement each other in an odd sort of way. I like Skeeter a lot, it's just that whenever he and Uncle Bubba are together, you have to keep an eye on them.

I was satisfied to leave the whole thing alone, confident in the fact that Aunt Irma was watching carefully over Uncle

Bubba's plans. In fact, I really didn't see either one of them until Easter Sunday morning at the service.

The church was packed, and it probably sat a full fifty people. I was sitting in one of the back pews when Aunt Irma came strutting over. "You're just not going to believe what Bubba's done for the cantata!" she said, her smile stretching across her face. "That precious man even stayed up late and prepared a couple of batches of wings for the luncheon afterwards! Lordy, that man did up some wonderful teriyaki wings, and a batch of lemon as well."

I'd seen the plywood tomb that he'd set up behind the choir loft when I came in, and there were several white plywood clouds hanging at the front. For Cut Plug, this was one major production.

I got worried when the cantata started and Uncle Bubba wasn't there, though. They went through the entire Easter pageant, all the way up to the resurrection, without a hitch. Mrs. Fenton's solo was even on key and well within the tempo that the choir director had set.

It came time for the angel to step out in front of the tomb to proclaim the blessed event, and everyone, including the choir, turned around to face Uncle Bubba's plywood display. The silence lasted longer than it should have.

I caught some motion over to the side of the whole setup, and I recognized Skeeter in his suit and ever-present gimmie cap. His slender frame was wrestling with a heavy rope, tugging on it for all he was worth.

Five seconds later, Uncle Bubba came crashing down from the plywood clouds, dressed in a white sheet with posterboard wings and a thick rope around his waist. Obviously he was supposed to be the angel who descended and declared the miracle, but in the few seconds that he was visible, it was apparent that Uncle Bubba had fallen asleep up there.

I guess he'd started cooking the chicken wings so late that he lost the necessary hours of slumber, or maybe the first part of the cantata was just that boring. Whatever the reason, Uncle Bubba fell a good ten feet onto the floor behind the choir, knocking the tomb off its supports and over onto the two pews in the choir loft.

The members of the choir were screaming as they scrambled into the congregation and out of danger, and this caused even more of a commotion among the people in attendance. A good many of the people were frozen to the pews in shock, while the others were running to the back of the church in a wild panic.

It woke Uncle Bubba up, though, and he just got to his feet and started singing his part in the cantata, like nothing had happened at all. His halo may have been slung to one side, and the angel wings were hanging way too low, but Bubba sang with all his heart and soul.

After he finished, the other choir members drifted back up to the front and continued their program. I have to say it was magnificent, even if Uncle Bubba had fallen asleep up in the plywood clouds.

Some people say this was the best Easter cantata ever, while the others at least have to admit it was the most interesting. Afterwards, when everyone adjourned to the all-purpose building that the church had built last year, Uncle Bubba stood behind his pans of wings, one teriyaki and another lemon, and served them right there in his angel costume. It was inspiring.

To catch a glimpse of that fine moment, you can make the wings with only a little trouble. Both can be prepared exactly the same way, which makes them easy to do at the same time. You'll be a real hero when you serve these wings—the angel costume is optional.

Angelic Lemon Wings

20 chicken wings
¼ cup soy sauce
¼ cup cooking sherry
½ cup lemon juice
1 Tbsp sugar
½ tsp salt
1 Tbsp ginger
1 Tbsp paprika

Uncle Bubba's angelic lemon wings can be prepared by using the same instructions as his famous teriyaki chicken wings.

Teriyaki Chicken Wings

20 chicken wings
1 cup teriyaki sauce
1 Tbsp brown sugar
1 tsp lemon juice
½ cup pineapple juice
2 garlic cloves, minced

For either one of these delectable recipes, combine all of the ingredients together in a bowl and submerge the wings in the mixture. Cover the bowl and put it in the refrigerator, where it should marinate for a few hours—or even overnight if you have time.

Preheat the oven to 375 degrees, and arrange the wings on a shallow cookie sheet. If you're doing both recipes at the same time, then use two different sheets, since the marinade will tend to run.

Bake the wings for 15 minutes, then take them out and brush them with the marinade. Put them back in for another 15, and repeat the process. Go ahead and discard the marinade.

After another 15 minutes, it's time to start checking them to see if they're ready. All ovens vary slightly, so use your best judgement, and enjoy the wings after they've cooled a little.

3

Pink Flamingo Sunday

Uncle Bubba was so impressed with his performance in the Easter cantata that he was at church bright and early for the next several weeks running, just in case someone still wanted to brag on his angel appearance or his chicken wings at the covered dish lunch.

The only problem with this was that since Aunt Irma sang in the choir, Bubba always ended up sitting with Mr. Patterson. To the casual observer, this might not have been a bad thing. Unfortunately, they had a bit of a history.

Mr. Patterson was easily twenty years older than my uncle and had worked on the same crew over at the cement plant as Bubba for as far back as I could remember. They weren't really friends and didn't have much in common, but they did share a love for practical jokes. When that unlikely pair teamed up, the world just wasn't a safe place to be in. They had truly terrorized the plant over the years. Every summer the *Sports Swimsuit* magazine from the men's room somehow got switched with the *Decorating Monthly* from the ladies' room. Every fall, a sack of birddog poop was set on fire right outside of the line supervisor's door for him to stomp right into.

But no one, least of all Aunt Irma, saw any problem with the two characters sitting together on the back row of the church all those Sundays. I found out later that they had hatched their plan right there during one of Pastor Frawley's more boring sermons and had begun saving their spending money for a solid month before pooling it and ordering a special package from some novelty shop all the way over in Dallas.

The pair got up in the wee hours of the very morning the Cut Plug Missionary Baptist Church was dedicating its new indoor baptismal pool. Everyone had heard how it was up at the front of the church behind the choir loft, with a big mural of the Jordan River painted on the back wall. Emerald plastic ivy lined both its sides, just like the banks of the river, and spilled from the front edge of the tank over onto the walnut paneling below.

The big Sanctification Sunday came, and the full eight-member choir stood there like the heavenly chorus in the choir loft in back of the preacher, with the deep blue velvet curtains drawn behind them. Right before the sermon, those regal folds were supposed to be pulled back to reveal the new baptismal fount.

The choir special was spectacular, at least as choir specials go at the Cut Plug Missionary Baptist Church. Their last note was still ringing in the air as they took their seats and Pastor Frawley stood up at the pulpit. His voice sounded out with the verses of the book of Matthew, chapter three, telling of Jesus' baptism by John the Baptist.

As he reached a crescendo, Deacon Randall stood right on cue, crept as quietly as he could behind the choir, and began to slowly draw the cord at one side of the curtain. The blue velvet parted, and there was the baptismal in all its glory, with seventeen plastic pink flamingos stuck in the ivy along the edges. It was a sight to behold.

The good pastor had no idea, of course, so he kept preaching like there was no tomorrow, moving smoothly through the early chapters of Matthew. The congregation couldn't help but giggle at the sight, though, and this perplexed Pastor Frawley to no end. The choir looked even more confused than he did, since, like the preacher, they had yet to turn around. Pastor Frawley and the choir members were sure the congregation was seeing the beautiful baptismal fount that they had the night before and were therefore genuinely perplexed.

About that time Aunt Irma happened to glance over at Uncle Bubba and Mr. Patterson. She saw that they were suppressing guffaws to the point they were about to explode. Their faces were beet red, and every time their eyes met it was another struggle to keep composure.

Aunt Irma came to the realization that something was very wrong in the baptismal about the same time as the other ladies in the Book of Ruth Bible class, and they all turned around together.

Before them, in all their splendor, were the plastic pink flamingos wading along the River Jordan. The old women started swooning from the sight—all except for Aunt Irma, that is. She locked her eyes onto Uncle Bubba, and that left eyebrow of hers raised up slowly.

She was beyond embarrassment and had just enough steam built that she jumped up and screamed, "Bubba!" at the top of her lungs. She tore out of the choir loft and headed for the pew in the back.

Uncle Bubba just started laughing all the louder and ran right out the back door of the church. While the congregation sat there in stunned silence, you could hear his howls and Aunt Irma's screams slowly fading into the distance. The pastor assessed the situation quickly and had a word of closing prayer.

When I left the church, I drove all over Cut Plug looking for my aunt and uncle, just to make sure they were both alright. I didn't find them, though, even when I stopped by their house. When I got there, I was greeted by a wonderful surprise as I opened the front door. An incredibly spicy aroma greeted me, so I naturally drifted back to the kitchen.

Uncle Bubba had apparently fixed a batch of his five-spice wings to eat after church, so I sat down and helped myself. As good as that man was with practical jokes, he was even better with that particular wing recipe. Uncle Bubba buys his five-spice powder at the grocery store in the Asian food section, and it's a unique blend of star anise, fennel, cinnamon, cloves, and pepper. All those together make one hecka'va good wing.

To see what his five-spice wings were like on that pink flamingo Sunday, I'd certainly recommend that you give them a try.

Exotic-as-a-Flamingo Five-Spice Wings

20 chicken wings
½ tsp ginger powder
½ tsp garlic powder
1 tsp five-spice powder
½ tsp hot sauce
1 Tbsp sesame oil
¼ cup soy sauce
⅛ cup cooking sherry

Mix all of the ingredients together, and marinate the wings overnight in the refrigerator using a covered container. Swirl the wings in the sauce right before bed, then again when you get up in the morning. Do it a few more times before cooking the wings, if possible.

Preheat the oven to 375 degrees, then spread the wings out on a cookie sheet . Bake the wings for 20 minutes, then remove them and baste them with the marinade. Return them to the oven and continue baking approximately 25 more minutes or until the wings are done. Sometimes Uncle Bubba will add a few *light* sprinkles of five-spice powder before serving, but use your own judgement.

4

Taking Credit Where Credit's Deserved

It wasn't long before my uncle's thoughts turned back to opening his restaurant. He decided that he needed a game plan for implementing his goal, so Uncle Bubba went to his favorite place for hiding or thinking: He went fishing.

I had dropped by that Saturday morning just as he was driving away, so he circled back and insisted that I accompany him. As Uncle Bubba put it, "Nephew, it's always better to have two brains workin' on a problem this serious." I figured I'd be able to pull in a few fish for supper if nothing else, so I climbed into the pickup and we took off.

It was only a couple of miles out of town to Bartdale Creek, so we had our hooks wet in no time at all. The waterway was a deep, slow-moving channel that opened up into the lake just a short distance away, and a reasonable fisherman could always count on pulling in a few—especially on such a warm spring day.

Uncle Bubba wasn't there for the fish, though. I could plainly see that he wasn't paying any attention to his casting, and even after I'd changed baits a dozen times he was still throwing in a simple, purple plastic worm.

He finally sighed heavily and sat down on the bank. "Nephew, I'm getting mighty worried about the wing restaurant. Since it's pretty obvious that banker Trickle isn't going to loan me the money, I'm going to have to come up with something on my own." He finished reeling in the lure, then slung it back out across the creek and started slowly winding it in. "There's just gotta be a way."

We fished in silence for a minute or two, until Uncle Bubba finally snapped his fingers so loud that it probably sent every fish in the vicinity dashing back for the lake. "I've got it!" A huge grin broke on his face, and he began reeling in that worm for all it was worth. When it hit shore he laid the rod down and started pacing, just like he always did when he was hatching a scheme.

I knew the gears were turning up in that mind of his, because every now and then he'd nod his head and say "Yep," just like he was agreeing with himself.

"C'mon, Nephew, we're goin' back to the house." He began furiously packing up all the tackle, then threw it all in the back of the pickup. I got in just as he floored it, and we arrived at his place in only a couple of minutes.

Uncle Bubba hopped out of the truck and hurried toward the house. "I don't mean to run you off, Nephew, but I've got work to do!"

It was certainly not the oddest behavior I'd ever seen him exhibit, so I just wrote it off to some anxiety over the restaurant and went on about my business.

Next morning, I thought it might be best if I drove on over and just made sure everything was okay. Sometimes Uncle Bubba's ideas got a little out of hand.

I was just stepping up onto the porch when Aunt Irma met me at the door. "Thank goodness you're here! Bubba's been up all night, and he won't tell me what he's doing!"

She had a worried look on her face, so I patted her on the shoulder and sent her off to church, assuring her that I'd look in on Uncle Bubba. I found him back in the den, sitting in the recliner that Aunt Irma had bought him for an anniversary present about ten years ago, his mouth covered in the reddish-orange telltale sign of his famous fires-of-hell hot wings. He was chomping his way through the ones that remained uneaten, grinning ear-to-ear. There was another empty plate nearby that had traces of something I thought I recognized as pineapple, so he had obviously run through a couple of batches over the course of the evening. Looking at him, I could tell that Uncle Bubba was extremely pleased with himself. He had a magazine open on his lap, and he was punching the numbers on the telephone with the hand that wasn't covered in hot sauce.

"Nephew!" he hollered across the room, hanging up the phone. "You should have come over earlier and helped me eat these! I've been having a wing restaurant celebration!"

I couldn't tell exactly what he was talking about because all I could see was a big heap of magazines at his feet, but my curiosity was now piqued. As I sat down beside Uncle Bubba, he nodded at the almost-empty plate and I took one of the wings. It was delicious—nice and spicy just like I expected. When he made the hot wings for Aunt Irma I knew that he had to tone them down some by using less hot sauce, but these babies were full power.

"Yep, I had an inspiration yesterday afternoon," he went on. "I was up all night working on the master plan for my restaurant."

I just nodded, teething the last of the succulent meat off the bone. Now, hearing the words *master plan* come out of Uncle Bubba's mouth was never a good thing. At this point, though, I didn't think Aunt Irma had anything to worry about—Uncle Bubba looked docile enough.

He sat up proudly. "I figured that I didn't need banker Trickle to make the loan, and I've been working on a different route all night. To celebrate, I fixed up some pineapple lemon wings, and when those were gone I made a batch of my fires-of-hell specials." His eyes kind of narrowed, and I could tell that he was getting ready to divulge his strategy. "See, Nephew, I drove over to Hinkley's Grocery and bought one copy of every single magazine that they had on the rack. Between all the ads in those and all the commercials on late-night TV, I've applied for exactly 361 credit cards! Combine all the credit that they're going to give me on them, and we're talking about enough money to float a restaurant in chicken wing sauce!" He grinned so big I thought his face was going to split in half.

I started coughing up hot sauce, burning my throat, mouth, and lips like I'd swallowed molten lava. When I finally regained my composure, all I could say was, "You did what?"

Uncle Bubba rared back like a proud papa. "Just consider the restaurant under way. I'm gonna have thousands of dollars to spend getting it ready to go."

I couldn't believe what I was hearing. "Uh, Uncle Bubba," I started.

He held up his hands to stop me. "Now I already know what you're thinking, Nephew, and I've taken it all into account. I'm sure that a few of these credit card companies may not want to get on board right away. Still, the ones that do are going to give me the cash that I need to get the ball rolling!" His smile was still bright enough to light the room.

I picked up a paper towel and wiped off my mouth. "Uncle Bubba, I hate to bring this up, but just who do you think the credit card companies are going to contact for a reference on you before sending you those cards?"

His smile suddenly faded, and he sat there for a minute looking kind of confused. I finally saw sober recognition dawn on his face. It just went blank, and he dropped his head down into his hands.

"Banker Trickle?" he mumbled through his fingers.

I sighed. "I'm afraid so."

Uncle Bubba just reached down at the side of the chair, grabbed the handle, and reclined all the way back. He lay there, staring at the ceiling, while I finished off the wings. As bad an idea as this one had been, I knew that my uncle was getting dead level serious about opening this restaurant. More ideas were sure to follow.

If you ever need a little inspiration yourself, the recipes for these two are simple. When preparing either type of wings, keep an eye on them to make sure they don't burn. While you're watching them, feel free to contemplate any of the mysteries of the universe that you have yet to solve—these wings may well provide you the answer. If not, crank up the hot sauce a bit on the next batch of the fires-of-hell wings. It always worked for Uncle Bubba.

Fires-of-Hell Hot Wings

20 chicken wings
1 8-oz can tomato sauce
1 tsp black pepper
2 Tbsp red pepper flakes
1 Tbsp garlic powder
1 Tbsp onion powder
1 tsp salt
2 Tbsp jalapeño peppers, finely chopped
4 Tbsp hot sauce (your favorite variety)

These are wonderfully easy to prepare. To get started, preheat the oven to 375 degrees, then mix all the ingredients except for the wings in a bowl. Coat a baking sheet with any no-stick cooking spray, then dip the chicken wings in the sauce and place them on the sheet. You may have to do some touch-ups and brush the sauce over the wings to fully coat them. Bake for 20 minutes, then take out the wings. Turn them over and brush completely with sauce again, then bake for about another 20-25 minutes.

Pineapple Lemon Wings

20 chicken wings
½ tsp salt
¼ tsp white pepper
4 Tbsp dry sherry
3 cups bread crumbs
3 eggs
4 slices pineapple, quartered
½ cup fresh lemon juice
½ cup water
5 Tbsp packed brown sugar
2 Tbsp butter

2 tsp cornstarch

2 tsp minced fresh ginger

You're going to need some sort of deep fryer for this recipe, but sometimes Uncle Bubba uses a deep skillet with a quarter inch of olive oil.

To prepare these, start out by combining the sherry, white pepper, and salt in a small bowl and rolling each wing in the mixture.

Get two more small bowls; break the eggs in one and whisk, then put the bread crumbs into the other bowl. Dip each wing piece into egg, then roll in bread crumbs.

Deep-fry the wings, a few pieces at a time, until they are golden brown and cooked inside.

While you are doing this, put the pineapple slices in a blender, then turn it to the liquefy setting. Add the water, lemon juice, brown sugar, butter, cornstarch, and ginger. Transfer the sauce from the blender to a pan and heat over medium-high heat, stirring until the sauce boils and slightly thickens. Finally, coat each completed wing with the sauce. These are a little messy, but they are scrumptious!

An Out-of-This-World Evening

I think Uncle Bubba was a little depressed about not having any funding for his chicken wing restaurant, because I didn't hear from him for a couple of weeks. I saw him at the cement plant a few times, but he seemed distracted. That worried me a little, so at the next break I went and found Skeeter and Buck hanging out at the vending machines and asked them to keep an eye on Uncle Bubba.

I knew that Skeeter was almost as crazy as my uncle, but I was hoping that Buck would be the catalyst in the equation. He was a big ol' fellow and one of the more sane of my uncle's friends, except when it came to deer hunting. Buck got his name from bagging a 16-pointer when he was only eight years old, and it had just kept going from there.

He was a conscientious hunter, mind you, and used every ounce of meat to feed his family. He had his own smokehouse in his backyard, and over the years he'd become quite the master of curing deer meat. The only problem was the horns.

Buck had mounted them everywhere: all though his house, inside and out; on the outside of his smokehouse; above the door in his garage. The most outrageous, however, was the rack he had mounted on the front of his pickup like a monstrous hood ornament. Other than those eccentricities, he was a fellow that I trusted to keep a cool head.

I left Uncle Bubba in their hands, and didn't think about it again until Aunt Irma gave me a call about a week later. She needed my help at a get-together that she was hosting in a couple of evenings.

Her Book of Ruth Bible class was having their annual spring party, and every year they took a group photo to hang up on their wall at church. This year Aunt Irma was hosting it, and since she had already told Bubba that he was banished to the garage for the duration of the party, my presence was required to snap the picture.

I went over to their house that evening, and the street was lined with the cars belonging to all the ladies—those decade-old classics like Caddies, Deuce-Quarters, and Lincolns. I immediately spotted Buck's pickup with those big horns mounted on front, and then I saw Skeeter's truck parked behind it, so I figured they were keeping Uncle Bubba company while he was sequestered out in the garage.

Aunt Irma met me at the door, and as I walked into their living room I was overcome by the smell of hair spray and perfume. The ladies were all wearing their best outfits for the photograph, and they had their hair piled high on top of their heads.

It didn't take me but a few minutes to get everyone organized and posed, and before they knew it I'd snapped a group photo that caught them in all their splendor.

They insisted that I stay for the Bible study and refreshments. Even though I didn't particularly care to, it was one of those times where I bowed to Aunt Irma's hospitality and just went ahead and agreed. Besides, I knew that she'd baked biscotti, and Aunt Irma was becoming quite the gourmet with those long Italian cookies. She'd been selling them at church bazaars and town celebrations for the last few months, and everyone was going crazy over them.

The Bible program actually turned out to be kind of nice. Mrs. Mable Matheson gave the devotional, sharing the wisdom of the book of Proverbs as the group listened intently and reverently. She finally closed and asked Mrs. Oralee Franklin to read the scripture before the prayer. At Mrs. Oralee's direction, we all held hands, and she opened the King James version and began to read in perfect diction from the book of Proverbs: *"In all labour there is profit: but the talk of the lips tendeth only to penury. The crown of the wise is their riches: but the foolishness of fools is folly."* Right about then, Bubba came busting through the front door. "By God, Irma!" he yelled. "Skeeter's been kidnapped by a flying saucer!"

The room was deathly silent, and the only noise at all was Buck's boots hitting the front porch as he ran in to join Uncle Bubba. Both had a scared, disheveled look about them, and I suspected the worst.

Uncle Bubba stepped into the middle of all those ladies and began his tale. "There we were, out back in the garage, with some wings cooking on the grill just a few yards from the door, when a bright light flooded the entire backyard! Me and Skeeter and Buck all ran out, of course, just to see what was happening. Right about that time, this beam of blue light locked onto Skeeter and pulled him up! Everything went dark, and we saw the thing fly off into the heavens!" The women still stood there like pillars of granite, just staring at him. "Don't you hear what I'm saying?" he pleaded. "Skeeter's gone!"

The pause in the room was heavy with silent accusation, and finally Mrs. Franklin stepped over to Uncle Bubba and sniffed. She turned to the group, her nose still in the air, and said, "I believe that I smell some of that demon liquor."

Aunt Irma's eyes widened. "Bubba?" she said, a little louder than normal. It was more of a threat than a question.

Uncle Bubba was gesturing wildly. "But Irma, I'm telling you that Skeeter's been kidnapped by aliens! Buck and me saw it!" Buck stood silently behind him, nodding his head.

Irma walked over to him. "Have you two been drinking?" she asked in that no-nonsense, accusatory tone that she had.

"Well," Bubba stammered, "I mean, we were fixin' some bourbon wings out on the grill, and maybe a few honey tequila specials, but nothing that you'd really count as drinkin'." I don't think that flew at all with Aunt Irma. I really believe that she and the rest of the Book of Ruth Bible class thought Bubba and Buck were three-sheets-to-the-wind drunk.

Uncle Bubba was so insistent, though, that Aunt Irma finally called Deputy Hernandez to come over and check everything out. He combed the area but didn't find anything but the leftover bottles of Kentucky bourbon and Mexican tequila in the garage, and that was enough for the ladies to sew the whole matter up.

Most everyone believed that those three started sipping on some of the spirits left over from preparing the wings and merely stumbled outside into the bright security light that's up on the pole between the house and the garage. It didn't matter, though, since Skeeter was still missing.

I joined the deputy in searching the area, but we couldn't find him. As I walked past the grill, I couldn't help but take some of those wings with me—a few of each type—they're a couple of my absolute favorite recipes that Uncle Bubba does. And who knows, if there really had been a flying saucer, maybe it was the wings that brought the extraterrestrial visitors to Texas. If you want to try a few experiments for yourself, the recipes are simple. Although their flavors are completely different, the preparation is exactly the same. You're going to love them both, and so will any "out of town" visitors that show up.

Bubba's Bourbon Wings

20 chicken wings
½ cup bourbon
½ cup brown sugar
½ cup soy sauce
½ tsp red pepper
½ tsp salt
½ tsp garlic powder
½ tsp powdered ginger
2 Tbsp dehydrated onion flakes

The bourbon wings are prepared just like the honey tequila wings recipe that follows, so refer to it if you'd like to try them. In fact, it makes them even easier to prepare together!

Honey Tequila Wings

20 chicken wings
1 cup soy sauce
1 cup tequila
½ cup cider vinegar
½ cup honey
¼ cup brown sugar
¾ cup ketchup
2 Tbsp pepper flakes
1 bunch chopped cilantro
½ cup olive oil
2 Tbsp black pepper
2 Tbsp powdered mustard
1 tsp dried thyme

Start with the wings in a glass bowl. If you're making both recipes, use two bowls, because they have to be prepared separately. Bubba was using the big glass bowl that came with Aunt Irma's mixer, but since that one got broke on the patio last summer, he'll use about anything in the pantry now. Combine all the ingredients together, and pour the mixture over the wings. Put the bowl in the refrigerator to marinate overnight. If your fridge is like mine, you may have to move things around to make room.

Next day, fire up the grill, put on the wings, and baste them with the marinade sauce once. After a couple of minutes, turn the wings over and baste the other side. You may want to repeat the process a couple of times. After that, throw the rest of the marinade out, and grill the wings until they're done.

The Return of Skeeter

Well, word about Skeeter spread around town that evening faster than God gets the news. People started showing up on Uncle Bubba's doorstep just to see if the story might be true.

Before long, in fact, there were several dozen folks wandering around outside the house. Some of them were laughing at Bubba and Buck, and there were a few poor souls who actually believed that the alien invasion was finally happening and the focal point of their attack was Cut Plug, Texas.

The Book of Ruth Bible class was holding a prayer vigil for Skeeter because they were convinced that he had fallen prey to his own inebriated folly rather than some insidious alien plot.

Aunt Irma slipped outside to find Bubba in the middle of all the excitement. Even in a crisis, she was the consummate hostess, and it was bothering her to no end that all these people were there and she hadn't baked enough biscotti to go around. If there was anyone who could pull off a culinary miracle, though, she knew it was Uncle Bubba. With that in mind, she asked him to whip up some more wings.

After all the searching and worry, along with half a pot of coffee, my uncle was thinking pretty clearly. He knew that even though he had some wings in the freezer that could be thawed out in the microwave, he was out of hot sauce, most of his special seasonings were running low, and there was definitely not a drop of alcohol left in the garage.

He pondered the situation for a minute and finally decided the time had come to try a quick recipe that had just popped into his head some time ago. He hadn't been able to summon the courage to try it before now, but with a tired, captive audience like the one waiting outside, he just couldn't resist.

Bubba rolled up his shirt-sleeves and went into the kitchen, emerging an hour later holding a big plate of cola chicken wings.

That fact alone took the focus off of aliens and flying saucers for a while, as everyone had to try a wing for themselves. It didn't surprise Bubba a bit that they were the hit of the evening. Armed with a couple of extras on a napkin, I went back to the search.

By three A.M. we'd thoroughly combed the area and could find no trace of the alleged abductee. The crowd had started thinning out, and Deputy Hernandez brought up the fact that someone should go over and tell Skeeter's mom.

Now Skeeter was probably the only grown man left in the state who lived with his mother, but that's only because that rambunctious ninety-year-old woman had been thrown out of the only two nursing homes in the county. That was one lady who wasn't ready to go quietly into old age, and so Skeeter had invited her to stay with him as long as she could still get around.

Once she found out that her son had potentially been kidnapped by beings from another planet, that old woman was liable to start an intergalactic incident all by herself—not to mention what could happen to the messenger who brought the news.

It was a sorry sight, if I do say so myself. The three of us stood out on the porch: Pastor Frawley, Deputy Hernandez, and myself. We were all nodding our heads in agreement that someone should make the trip over to break the news, but not a single one of us was stepping up to the plate.

We were still weighing the situation when the Bible class broke up for the evening. It was later than many of those ladies had stayed up in the last twenty years, so even with all the adrenaline produced by praying for Skeeter, they were about to fade for the evening.

We gave our well wishes as they filed by and then turned our attention back to the subject of Skeeter's mother. We stood there in awkward conversation, trying to find a volunteer. It was five full minutes before the screaming started.

Mrs. Oralee Franklin had apparently driven about a block before she suddenly stopped and leapt out of her car. The three of us jumped off the porch and hit the ground running as fast as we could, but she still met us about halfway, yelling and flailing her arms in a frenzy. It may have been all the talk about aliens and such, but she was in a state of panic, claiming that they had come for her!

We approached the car cautiously. The deputy had his flashlight in one hand and his pistol in the other, so we felt pretty safe. As we got to the car the back door on the driver's side began to open slowly.

I couldn't see inside, but there was definitely something strange going on there. The deputy held his flashlight on the back window, and as the door swung completely open, Skeeter poured out of the back seat onto the pavement.

He stumbled a bit, like he was having a problem focusing, then he finally stood erect. He looked around, and the first word he said was, "Bubba?"

Skeeter was just as shocked as the rest of us. When Deputy Hernandez started asking about flying saucers, beams of light, and so forth, Skeeter stood there with a mystified look on his face. As it turned out, he didn't recall many events that night after Uncle Bubba's mason jar had made its way around a few dozen times.

Most people figured they had seen the security light and taken that for a spaceship, but to this day, Uncle Bubba and Buck both swear that the town of Cut Plug had been visited by aliens. Skeeter can't remember a thing, of course, but that just fuels the fire. Bubba says they messed with his brain.

No matter what happened, the cola wings Uncle Bubba came up with were fantastic. I made him write down the recipe right then and there, before he joined Skeeter in explaining everything to the deputy.

Soda-Pop Cola Wings

20 chicken wings
1 cup catsup
⅔ cup cola
1 cup brown sugar
1 tsp garlic salt
1 tsp onion salt
1 Tbsp soy sauce

Combine all of the ingredients together and spread them over the wings in as small a container as possible, to get maximum coverage. Marinate them for several hours in the refrigerator, if possible. If not, at least let them soak while you're getting ready to cook them.

Prepare your grill, light the fire, and let the coals get just right for cooking. Uncle Bubba always cooks on the down side of the fire, which means that he lets all the coals go to gray. Bring out the wings, brushing every 10 minutes with the sauce. Keep turning them, and stop adding marinade about 10 minutes before they're done.

This is one of those recipes that turn out to be just as delicious when prepared in the oven, so if it's cold or rainy outside, you should feel confident that the wings will be every bit as delicious. Just bake them at 375 degrees for approximately 45 minutes, basting every 10 minutes or so.

The Great Income Tax Audit

A week or so after all the flying saucer commotion had died down, I had just finished my shift at the plant and had nearly made it to my car, when I looked up to see Uncle Bubba roaring up in his pickup. It didn't take me any time at all to realize that he was in a cold-sweat panic over something.

"Nephew!" he hollered while he rolled down the driver's side window. "I'm in trouble, and I need your help somethin' fierce!"

While it wasn't that far a stretch to imagine my uncle being in trouble, the fact that he was asking me to be part of it was a little alarming. I hope I didn't sound a little hesitant when I said, "What ya got, Uncle Bubba?"

He held up a brown envelope with an official seal for the return address and one of those prepaid government markings for the stamp. "It's the IRS, Nephew. I'm being audited."

Those were serious words indeed. I nodded, waved him on, and followed my uncle to his house. When he got out of the truck he was rubbing the edges of that envelope and running his fingers over it again and again, like he wasn't sure whether it was a death sentence or a reprieve from the governor. In either case, it appeared like he was too afraid to peek inside.

I walked over and slapped him on the shoulder, doing my best to comfort him. "So exactly what in the world is going on with the IRS?"

He just shook his head. "I can't figure. Lord knows, I've never had anything happen like this before. Course, this was the first year I let Mr. Abernathy over at the feed store do my taxes."

It didn't surprise me that this was a new experience for my uncle—people in Cut Plug just didn't get audited. Everyone worked at the cement plant, the only charity that anyone gave to was the church, and the combined cash flow of the entire town wasn't enough for a big city accountant to sneeze at.

What did surprise me, though, was the part about Mr. Abernathy. That old man had run the feed store for as far back as I could remember, and no telling how long before that. The surprise must have been apparent on my face, because Uncle Bubba cleared his throat and started explaining.

"See, I was in the feed store last November to get some new overalls, and old Mr. Abernathy started telling me how he was going to do income tax services out of the store. Since he's treated me so good all the time I've been coming in there, I just thought I'd throw him our tax return this year to help him get started."

I waited a second, then asked the inevitable question. "So, Uncle Bubba, Mr. Abernathy does have some credentials to prepare returns, right?"

He shrugged. "Don't know. He just said that he was going to start doing them."

My worst fears were realized. Uncle Bubba had turned his yearly financial responsibilities over to some cowboy who was flying by the seat of his pants with tax forms that he probably picked up at the post office.

Uncle Bubba went on to explain to me that Mr. Abernathy had requested that I accompany them to the IRS office, which was located at the county seat. I had to take a vacation day to do that, but of course, I'd do anything for my Uncle Bubba. When they picked me up, Uncle Bubba's pickup smelled delicious, and I saw the plastic container in the floorboard.

He must have seen me looking down at it, because Uncle Bubba said, "I fixed some wings for the tax man this morning!"

That struck me as one of the worst ideas he'd ever had. "Uh, Uncle Bubba," I started.

"Now I know what you're thinking, Nephew," he interrupted. "This isn't a bribe, it's just a gift. I know how those IRS people are, so I fixed a batch of the most delicious, but easiest and cheapest wings in the world: my ranch style wings."

I climbed into the cab, squeezing Mr. Abernathy between us, trying my best not to step on the wing box. "Uncle, why don't we just leave these in the truck, at least at the first. We don't want any misunderstandings with these folks."

Uncle Bubba looked a little hurt, but Mr. Abernathy nodded his agreement, so we all drove down to the county seat together, mostly in silence. As Bubba parked the truck, the only advice that old Mr. Abernathy offered us was, "When we get in there, just follow my lead." I can't tell you how disturbing that was to my ears.

We traversed the hallways of the courthouse building and arrived at the county IRS office intact. We only had to wait twenty minutes for the auditor to finish lunch before starting Uncle Bubba's session. The three of us filed humbly in and sat in the uncomfortable metal chairs in front of the auditor's desk and waited for him to join us. A placard resting on the edge simply said *Mr. Birdy Thomas—Internal Revenue Service*.

As we sat there in those horrible seats waiting for the auditor to complete his lunch and join us, Mr. Abernathy looked carefully around the room, then whispered softly, "Now, Bubba, if there are any questions about your son, I want you to just point over at your nephew there."

His statement hit me like a cement truck. "What? Uncle Bubba doesn't have any kids!" My voice was loud enough that the old fellow snapped his head around, pursed his mouth, and shushed at me. Bubba just sat there staring straight ahead, his eyes as wide as hubcaps.

"Oh Lord, we're all going to jail," Uncle Bubba muttered under his breath.

Mr. Abernathy sat up in his chair and straightened his tie. "Bubba, there ain't nobody going to jail. You just follow my lead."

His words didn't seem to ease my uncle's feelings any, though. He just sat there looking dead on at the wall, like a deer caught in the headlights of a diesel on some county road.

Mr. Abernathy snapped his fingers. "Oh yeah, and if he mentions your business, just act sad that you lost all that money last year."

I was starting to get angry. "Business? Uncle Bubba doesn't have a business!" I glared at Abernathy.

He held his hands up to stop me. "Your uncle said that he was wanting to start a chicken wing restaurant. I just gave him a little bit of a head start."

"Oh Lord, we're all going to jail," Uncle Bubba said again, his gaze transfixed.

Mr. Abernathy shook his head. "We are not going to jail, Bubba, trust me."

I couldn't believe what was happening. It was the IRS we were messing with, and there was no telling what Abernathy had actually done. I pointed my finger right at him. "If you get my uncle into any trouble at all, you're going to answer to me."

He shushed me again. "Just be quiet now, and everything will be fine. One more thing, though." He seemed a little hesitant, so I knew that it wasn't going to be good. "I put down that Bubba's son had a hearing problem for the extra deduction, so if you could, act like you can't hear a thing that's going on."

My uncle was visibly shaking now. "Oh Lord, we're all going to jail." Uncle Bubba seemed to be singularly focused on that one very real possibility.

Mr. Abernathy looked over and hissed, "Bubba, stop saying that!"

For a fleeting moment, I wondered if our only out might be for Uncle Bubba to ply that auditor with the ranch style wings, but I quickly dismissed it. We were already in enough trouble.

The door creaked open, and the IRS agent entered the room. Mr. Thomas was a lemon-faced, puckered-up fellow who seemed to think he already had a handle on his little world. Unfortunately, his little world now included Uncle Bubba. We sat in uncomfortable silence while he read over my uncle's tax return, giving an occasional "hmmm..." or "ah-ha!"

I'll tell you, I was convinced that my uncle was a goner. If I never have to sit through another tax audit, that will be too soon for this Texas boy. Finally, Mr. Thomas laid the return down on his desk, then turned it around to face Uncle Bubba.

"It seems we have a slight problem here," the man began. I don't know about my uncle and Mr. Abernathy, but my butt cheeks were clenched up tighter than banker Trickle's wallet.

"It seems that you failed to sign your return." The auditor offered Uncle Bubba a pen, but he just sat there staring at it.

"Oh Lord," Uncle Bubba said, in a state that was almost catatonic.

Mr. Abernathy quickly took the pen and placed it in Uncle Bubba's hand. "My client is simply saying, Oh Lord, how did he miss something that simple." He almost had to guide my uncle's hand as he signed the form.

Mr. Thomas took the form, examined the signature, and grunted. I took this as a sign that we had successfully completed our mission, so I tugged on Uncle Bubba's arm until he got up and walked out of the office with us.

I don't think I've ever seen Uncle Bubba that scared, because he didn't say a word all the way back to Cut Plug. Mr. Abernathy and I opened the package of wings and finished them off long before we hit the city limits.

After we dropped Abernathy off at his feed store out on the highway, I made Uncle Bubba promise that he would never trust his income tax return to anyone other than himself or a licensed preparer. He was more than happy to agree to that.

On the drive back to his house, Uncle Bubba started getting his wits about him again, and he said the first thing that made sense this entire trip: "Nephew, I don't think there's any reason to worry your aunt with all this IRS business."

I couldn't have agreed more.

Now while I don't advocate bribery, had it come to that, Uncle Bubba's ranch style wings would have been some serious ammunition. You may want to keep the recipe handy, just in case.

Ranch Style Wings

20 chicken wings
3 Tbsp ranch dressing (regular or no-fat)
½ cup bread crumbs
½ tsp paprika
½ tsp white pepper
¼ tsp salt

Preheat your oven to 375 degrees, then put the ranch dressing in a small bowl and coat each chicken wing. In another bowl, mix the bread crumbs and seasonings thoroughly, then coat each wing with the mixture. Spray a cookie sheet with a no-fat vegetable spray, and bake for about 45 minutes until the wings are done.

The part that Uncle Bubba would've missed with the IRS agent makes them taste the best, though: Serve the wings with a side of additional ranch dressing.

8

The Return Visit

*U*ncle Bubba certainly knew that he didn't have to buy my silence about the income tax business, but nevertheless he invited me over a week later for an evening with another of my favorites from his arsenal of recipes: orange citrus barbecue wings. It sounded strange every time I told someone about those wings, but they were truly delicious.

I sat down at the table that night to a wonderful meal, and all Uncle Bubba could talk about was his wing restaurant and how he might be able to finance it. Aunt Irma rolled her eyes more than once during the course of it all.

It was certainly easy to see how seriously he was taking the subject, and I knew that if there was any possible way in the world, the chicken wing restaurant was going to be a reality someday. In the meantime, though, my plan was simply to keep Uncle Bubba's wild ideas in check, while lending as much of a helping hand as I could.

We finished off a good portion of the wings, and they were as delicious as any that Uncle Bubba had ever prepared. Enough of a pile was left over, though, that I was secretly hoping Uncle Bubba would send them home with me.

I had started clearing off the table when Aunt Irma insisted on doing it herself, just like always. She quickly shooed Uncle Bubba and I off to the den, and so we hustled out of her way.

Bubba was in his favorite chair, spinning schemes and ideas, when my aunt came in carrying her sewing kit and an armload of soft blue material. "C'mon, Bubba, help me out with this dress." She popped the bundle out, and it expanded into a beautiful garment indeed. It was a simple but elegant dress, sky blue in color. Its softly billowing sleeves ended in delicate three-inch cuffs with pearl-colored buttons. I wasn't exactly one for fancy clothes, but that was one stunning outfit.

The front was adorned with little white lace, and it flowed into a soft gathered waist. I just knew Aunt Irma was going to look beautiful in it.

My uncle didn't even stop his train of thought, keeping up his current speculation into whether or not he had contributed enough money to the pension fund at work to pay for the restaurant if he drew it out early. He was obviously used to being pressed into service as a dress dummy.

Uncle Bubba held his arms out, and Aunt Irma carefully slipped the sleeves over them and then gently pulled the dress up to him. Now there is a significant size difference between the two of them, and Bubba's stomach pooched the middle of the dress out to make it look more like a fancy delivery gown in the obstetrics ward than Sunday attire.

She couldn't button the cuffs, of course, or even begin to pull it far enough around Bubba to think about zipping it up in back. It was apparently good enough for her to check the hem, though, because she dropped to her knees with the sewing kit. I kind of drifted from listening to my uncle's speculations, to watching my aunt's expert craftsmanship. She had half a dozen straight pins tucked firmly between her lips, and her fingers were moving magically along the bottom of the garment.

My attention suddenly snapped back to Uncle Bubba, because he had abruptly stopped talking and had a strange look on his face. Just then, I noticed it, too. The room was getting brighter.

In a hushed voice, my uncle whispered, "They've come back."

I turned slowly, and there was a light coming in from the window that was as brilliantly white as I've ever seen. It was getting brighter and brighter, and I could feel the hairs on the back of my neck standing straight up.

Aunt Irma just sat there frozen, but Uncle Bubba was on the move, the delicate, blue dress flapping around him. I think he had taken so much ribbing about the flying saucer incident that he was determined to get absolute proof this time.

"Nephew!" he called back over his shoulder, creeping toward the door. "Irma! Ya'll come on!"

I helped Aunt Irma to her feet, and we caught up with him at the door. He turned his head slightly, still keeping an eye on the window, and whispered, "Get ready. This may not be the easiest thing to see, but they're here. It's the aliens that took Skeeter."

With that, he threw open the door and rushed outside onto the front lawn. We followed closely behind, a little apprehensive perhaps, but willing to back Bubba to the end.

"Irma! Nephew! There it is! Those aliens have come back for me!" Bubba was jumping up and down, pointing at something, and the motion of the dress was just a few seconds behind that of his body. That made the fancy blue dress keep oscillating with his stomach, even after he stopped. I couldn't decide whether my aunt was scared of the aliens, or simply worried about what Uncle Bubba was doing to her dress.

My eyes followed the direction that Uncle Bubba was pointing. There in front of us, hovering in all its alien mystery and beauty, was the spacecraft from another world.

Only, it looked suspiciously like Mr. Patterson's four-wheel-drive hunting truck. The row of spotlights mounted on top of the cab were all on, aimed at the house, and that old man must have slowly eased his truck up toward the window to get the spaceship effect.

A tremendous roar of laughter exploded, as the folks from my uncle's crew at the cement plant bailed out of the bed of the

truck. Mr. Patterson hopped out of the cab, and when he saw Bubba in the dress, he howled even louder.

Uncle Bubba turned twenty-three shades of red before he began to chuckle himself. Before I knew it, he had joined in and was laughing with more vigor than anyone in the yard. He finally clapped Mr. Patterson on the back, congratulating him for one of the best pranks of the year.

To Aunt Irma's horror, Bubba was frolicking around in the dress out there in the front yard, having as good a laugh at himself as anyone on his crew. My uncle sure knew when to admit that someone had gotten the best of him, and how to play it out with dignity. Even in a sky blue, fancy dress.

The whole group finally filed into the house, where Bubba offered everyone a round of the leftover orange citrus barbecue wings. He paraded all around the den, serving them in Aunt Irma's beautiful garment, and she just followed right behind him every step of the way, fussing about how he was ruining her dress.

Everyone had a great time and agreed that those wings were spectacular. Even Mr. Patterson had to admit that Uncle Bubba had upstaged the prank. While I can't speak to his method of serving the orange citrus barbecue wings, I can assure you that those wings were delicious.

Orange Citrus Barbecue Wings

20 chicken wings
⅓ cup chili sauce
¼ cup orange marmalade
1 Tbsp red wine vinegar
1½ tsp Worcestershire sauce
¼ tsp garlic powder
¼ tsp powdered mustard

Combine all the ingredients together in a bowl, and submerge the wings in the mixture. Marinate them overnight or at least for several hours. When you're ready to cook them, preheat your oven to 375 degrees. Remove the wings from the marinade, shaking off any excess, and put them on a cookie sheet that has been coated with a vegetable spray. Bake the wings for a total of 45 minutes to an hour or until they are done. Every 15 minutes remove the wings and brush them with the marinade.

Aunt Irma always goes on about how healthy these are because they contain vitamin C from the presence of the orange, but I've never put any stock in that—I just think they're great!

Cut Plug Memorial Day

Memorial Day was fast approaching in Cut Plug, and I knew what that meant. The same thing happened every year: Uncle Bubba fought the city council for the right to organize a parade.

I don't know if there was a more patriotic soul in Cut Plug than Uncle Bubba, and it was one of his dreams in life to have a Memorial Day parade down Main Street to honor all the veterans from our small town. Unfortunately, Mr. Anester, the city attorney, was too concerned with the possibility that some accident might libel the city. It weighed on him far heavier than paying homage to anyone who had fought for our country. His impassioned speeches to the city council always got the parade voted down. After all those years, I think it had become more important to Mr. Anester to beat Uncle Bubba than to protect the city's interests. He had a record going that he wasn't about to let go of. For whatever reason he had, this year had been no different.

My uncle wasn't in the mood to talk when I got to his house after the city council meeting. In fact, he just stood out in the driveway, leaning against the side of his pickup, staring off into space. Sensing that he wanted to be alone, I just left him to his own thoughts. I knew the story about Uncle Bubba that most people didn't.

If you were to ask Uncle Bubba what he did in the service, he'll tell you that he was the best danged cook in the Marines and just leave it at that. There's a little more to it, though.

Uncle Bubba wasn't a cook; he was a lieutenant during the worst part of the Vietnam War. He saw the things that ate away at the souls of men like a cancer, and somehow he survived it all. He never talked about it with me, but one time we drove a few counties over to the Veteran's Hospital to visit a fellow named Mr. Belton from his old unit. While Uncle Bubba went down to the cafeteria to sneak a cheeseburger upstairs for his friend, that man shared a tale with me that I will never, ever, forget.

As the story went, a chopper had dropped Bubba and the five other men in his patrol at the very edge of occupied territory. Their mission was to breach the North Vietnamese line and report back on enemy strength and readiness in the area.

They were supposed to be out for twelve hours, but during the course of their mission, the divisions on the map suddenly changed. The enemy had advanced the lines considerably, and Bubba and his team were trapped far away from any safe landing zone or refuge.

Communication was sparse on the radio, but the patrol got the idea pretty soon. All they could do was press southward, hoping for a miracle. In a few days, they were ragged and starving, expecting to see the enemy pouncing out on them with every small jungle sound they heard. As they slowly made their way south, Bubba took it on himself to go out in the wee hours to scavenge for food.

Sometimes he returned with a partial meal that he'd stolen from a nearby village, or a small animal that he managed to trap, or even an armful of some vegetation that he had deemed edible. It wasn't always a gourmet feast, but it kept the men alive and their spirits sound.

Mr. Belton told me how Bubba would make a huge production out of cooking the meal, no matter how meager it was. He made up tales of fancy restaurants, hoity-toity waiters, and unreasonable dress codes to entertain the others. His antics fed their morale as much as their stomachs, and it gave them the drive to keep pressing onward.

The unit had been out six days when the unthinkable happened: They crossed paths with a Viet Cong patrol. It was a total shock for them all, and the melee of bullets that ensued took its deadly toll. There were casualties on both sides, and when the remaining Viet Cong finally fled, Uncle Bubba's unit was down to only three: Bubba, Mr. Belton, and Charlie Anderson. I will always remember hearing the names of the others, who perished on that day: Edwards, Jefferson, and Waterston. The surviving members of the patrol carried the others' bodies in a dead run for as long as they possibly could, and when they found a clearing where they felt safe, three funerals were held. They were given as much of a hero's send-off as could be mustered in those conditions; they were buried with honor and prayer.

After paying their final respects to their fallen brethren, the survivors continued on. They periodically tried to radio for a chopper, but their appeals were met only with static. It was an hour before Uncle Bubba realized that Anderson had been wounded as well, but he had been hiding it so as not to slow them down.

They each knew that stopping might give the Viet Cong a chance to catch up, so they continued on their journey southward. Charlie Anderson grew weaker by the hour, and Uncle Bubba finally lifted him up onto his back and carried him. The man fell unconscious, and by the time that they stopped for the evening, my uncle sadly discovered that he had died at some point along the way.

Bubba and Mr. Belton held a final funeral, then a few days later walked out of the jungle to a clear landing zone where they were able to radio for extraction. Mr. Belton said that after the chopper took them to the new base, Uncle Bubba didn't talk to anyone at all for a few days. It apparently took him months to resolve whatever inner demons remained from losing his buddies.

Mr. Belton's story touched me and let me see a dimension of my uncle that might have otherwise remained hidden. I looked at him a bit differently then, as he came bursting through that hospital door with a cheeseburger and fries tucked discreetly away in a paper sack from the hospital cafeteria. That was one incredible day.

As I looked back at him in his driveway, I knew that whole thing must have still been weighing on my uncle's mind as he stood there, leaning up against his pickup.

On the evening before Memorial Day, he called and told me that he'd be grilling wings out in the backyard and that I was welcome to stop by whenever I wanted.

I woke up early the next day and decided that I'd give him a hand getting the grill ready. I was on my way over to Uncle Bubba's house when I happened to glance over and see a few trucks parked by the town square. I recognized Bubba's and Skeeter's and of course Buck's pickup with those deer horns mounted on the front of the hood. I decided I'd better circle around and see what was going on.

As I pulled up, Uncle Bubba had just hoisted the Stars and Stripes to the top of the pole in the middle of the square. He was dressed in his Marine uniform, and while it didn't fit by any stretch of the imagination, he still carried it with a large degree of dignity. Skeeter and Buck stood there with their hands over their hearts as Bubba reached inside the open window of his pickup and pushed a button on the tape deck.

The solemn bars of "Taps" rang through the air, and my Uncle Bubba turned to the flagpole and gave our nation's banner a full-blown military salute. I watched him stand there at attention while the notes rang out, tears streaming down his face.

I found some solace in the fact that Mr. Anester wouldn't allow a parade, because I don't think Bubba's friends could have been given a more memorable tribute than I had witnessed that day. Although they had fallen in a foreign land, their memory was alive and well in Cut Plug, Texas. Thank God for people like my uncle.

I followed the trio back to Uncle Bubba's house, where we stood around the grill in silence as he prepared the wings. On some occasions, you just have to just sit back and reflect on the more important things in life.

The Honorable Order of the Armadillo

June came roaring into Cut Plug with a vengeance, its hot breath burning away any remaining cool spring breezes. The residents all turned their air conditioners on early even for Texas. You could walk outside and hear the compressors humming up and down the streets. In only a few days, the window units were already dripping water that condensed into small puddles on the ground. It was one of the early summer rituals, though, that I'd come to expect and embrace. At the time I didn't realize there were other rituals, dark and secret, laying in wait for me.

I had been to the local grocery to pick up a few supplies for the weekend, when I was ambushed in my driveway. A cloth was thrown over my head as I opened the door of my pickup, but the panic lasted only for a second, since Uncle Bubba's voice came booming through the confusion.

"Don't be scared, Nephew! You've just been nominated to be a member of the Honorable Order of the Armadillo! Just sit back and enjoy the initiation ceremony."

I knew that my uncle had been a member of the local lodge at least as long as I'd been alive. The prospect of joining had never crossed my mind, though. I was certainly apprehensive about it now, of course, as I was being led blindly away from my house.

I bumped into what only could be a full rack of deer horns, so I assumed that Buck's pickup was being used to transport me. "Hello, Buck," I said. There was only a confused silence, and I figured that they were wondering how to respond.

Uncle Bubba finally shushed me, saying, "Nephew, these are secret proceedings that you're being brought into. Just hush up for now."

I didn't say anything else, because I hated to burst Uncle Bubba's balloon. The Honorable Order of the Armadillo was perhaps the most exposed secret lodge in the country. Over the years, the wives of the lodge members had slowly extracted information from their husbands and compared notes. It was no great mystery that the Armadillos met on the second Tuesday of every month in Junior Newton's barn. Everyone also knew that Bubba was the Grand Dillo this year, and that Skeeter was the recording secretary. The one thing that no one could figure out, though, was what went on in the Armadillo meetings every month.

Once I was crammed into Buck's truck blindfolded, between him and Bubba, I figured I was about to find out.

We were on the road for a good ten minutes, just about the right distance over to Junior's. I started to bring up the fact that I had one grocery bag back in my truck with milk, cheese, and a couple of frozen dinners that was certainly going to spoil by the time all this nonsense was over. Uncle Bubba was probably having such a good time with it all, though, that I decided it wasn't worth mentioning. Instead, I sat back and enjoyed the ride.

When we reached our destination, the fellows helped me out of the truck, and I could tell that I was being led inside a building. I still couldn't see a thing. The huge barn door was slammed shut behind us, and the cloth was removed from my head. Before me was one of the strangest sights my eyes had ever seen.

Thirty or forty men stood there in rows, all decked out in knee-length purple robes with bright gold trim. That wasn't the unnerving part. What really got me was the fact that on the head of every single one of them was a cap like the legendary Daniel Boone wore. But instead of raccoons, these were real armadillos, head and all. It felt like all those beady little black eyes on the caps were staring right at me. I couldn't help but yell out and jump back a step or two.

"What the hell are you fellas wearin'?" was all I could think to say.

No one even cracked a smile, and finally Uncle Bubba said, "This is the official Honorable Order of the Armadillo ceremonial uniform, Nephew." He proudly squared his shoulders back. "And just think, if you pass initiation, you're going to get to wear one of these, too!"

I'm not sure if that announcement had the effect on me that my uncle thought it would. The idea of even being caught dead in one of those get-ups wasn't appealing. I studied them closer and began to notice subtle differences. Some of the men wore golden sashes over the robe, while others had pins of different shapes, colors, and sizes on what would ordinarily be the left breast pocket if the robes were to have pockets. A few people had large gold stripes circling their lower sleeves, and I noticed that Uncle Bubba had four. Must have had something to do with his rank of Grand Dillo, I supposed.

I was still sizing up those outfits when something that my uncle had said struck me: He had mentioned the word *initiation*. I gave him a suspicious look and slowly asked, "So how does a fellow get initiated to the Honorable Order of the Armadillo, Uncle Bubba?"

He hummed and hawed for a second and finally confessed, "Well, Nephew, we haven't really had that many new members since we started the lodge, so that part's kind of up in the air

right now. We did appoint a membership committee to study the situation, though."

Skeeter stepped forward from the crowd. "That's right, and I'm thinking what we ought to do is to line up in two long rows and have you run between us while we smack you with paddles." There were mixed reviews to his suggestion, with some of the guys nodding their heads in agreement, while others were looking at Skeeter like he'd lost his mind.

It didn't take me a second to decide which side of the fence I was going to fall on for that idea. "Skeeter, ain't nobody going to hit me with a paddle. Now just get that out of your mind right now."

Mr. Patterson worked his way to the front. "Well, son, I've got an idea for you. What if we dressed you up like a woman, drove you into the next county, and made you hitchhike back to town?" I have to give it to that old man, he was certainly an original thinker. There was no way in the world I was going to do that either, of course, but it was an original idea. I just shook my head to let them know that suggestion was out of the question.

Uncle Bubba finally stepped up and said, "I've got it! I was going to make some of my pepper wings anyway, so what if I grill them up right now, extra peppery, and we make my nephew eat the whole batch without a drop of water to drink!" There were a few snickers around the room, even a couple of guffaws, and the merit of the idea caught on swiftly.

He'd done me a favor, of course. My uncle knew I could eat his hottest wings with only a smile to go with them, but that wouldn't be necessary today. To everyone there, the challenge seemed ominous. I knew that the pepper wings weren't his hottest by any stretch of the imagination. They were delicious, and to watch them being prepared with all those pepper varieties you'd think they would be hotter than a Cut Plug summer. In reality, they were packed full of flavor and were actually pretty mild.

Uncle Bubba was sporting a wide grin, playing the whole thing up. "I don't want us to have to suffer like my nephew will, so I'll fix the rest of us up some fiery lemon wings!" There was a chorus of approving voices. "You know," Uncle Bubba continued, for those of you who don't want any heat at all, I'm even going to whip up some rosemary wings that won't be as punishing!" Uncle Bubba gave everyone a wink, then set out about his business.

He quickly lit the grill and began preparing the wings, and while we were waiting, Skeeter informed me that I would be required to craft my own armadillo hat. I wasn't that keen on even owning such a thing. Like I'd said before, the head was intact, with the eyes of the armadillo staring over the forehead of the wearer. The full body made up the bulk of the hat, and the armored tail hung down in back. All in all, I think a much better symbol for the lodge could have been chosen.

Skeeter went on. "As an Armadillo-candidate, you may seek the wisdom of three lodge members for the method of securing your armadillo hat." He spread his arm out, gesturing across the group.

Mr. Patterson was still standing out front, so I pointed to him first. He paused a second, hitched up his britches, and struck a scholarly pose. "Ya' see, son, the thing that you want to do is trap your prey. It doesn't take much to build the trap, then bait it out in a field. After only a few days, you'll have a 'dillo in there that you can take over to Little Ernie's Taxidermy shop." From the middle of the crowd, I saw Little Ernie Fratwhiler nod his head in agreement, thankful for the plug. Little Ernie was given his moniker to distinguish him from his father, Big Ernie Fratwhiler. It was an irony of nature that Little Ernie weighed in at a clean three hundred pounds.

Out of the corner of my eye I saw Buck grimacing like Mr. Patterson had spoken heresy. I thanked the old man, then nodded my head toward Buck. He didn't waste a second stepping up with his solution. "Now I don't know what sort of man would insist on trapping his prey, but I'd strongly recommend that you do the only humane thing and hunt the varmint down with a rifle." He strutted out to the front of the group, walking around like he was Socrates teaching philosophy to a new pupil. "Course, you're going to need to use your night-vision scope."

"Uh, Buck, I don't have a night-vision scope," I interjected. He looked at me like I had broken out in some foreign tongue.

"No night-vision scope? Hell, you can't even call yourself a hunter if you don't have a night-vision scope." He stopped for a minute and just shrugged. "Well, you can borrow mine then. Anyway, you set up beside one of the county roads and just wait. Pretty soon, you'll see one of those boogers skipping across the highway. All you have to do is get him in the cross hairs, and that fellow'll be attending the next meeting sitting on top of your head."

It wasn't that appealing a suggestion, but as he offered his solution I couldn't help but notice that Skeeter was sliding into the back, just like he didn't want anyone to notice him. It made me curious enough to point at him for my final pick. "Okay, Skeeter, tell me how you got your armadillo."

He just stood there in the back and said, "Either one of those ways would be just fine. I'd suggest that you go with one of them."

The members of the Honorable Order of the Armadillo were all looking at each other with puzzled glances, probably wondering, as I was, what Skeeter had done. This was too good to pass up. "No, Skeeter, I'm asking how you got your armadillo. You said I could ask three lodge members—well, you're my third."

He stood there nervously for a second, then said something under his breath. Everyone was curious now, and Buck wrinkled up his brow and said "What?"

"'89 pickup!" Skeeter yelled. "Okay, okay! I drove up and down the road in front of my house all night until I hit one!" He slinked down onto a nearby bale of hay as silence blanketed the barn.

The Armadillos exchanged quizzical glances, until the quiet was broken by Uncle Bubba's cry, "The initiation pepper wings are ready for the pledge!"

I dug right in and enjoyed them, and made it through the evening with the Armadillos. I ate my pepper wings, making painful faces all the while for the benefit of the fellows. The fiery lemon wings and rosemary wings were a hit as well—the brother Armadillos wolfed them down. As they did, they explained how

I could order my uniform from the Heavenly Medley Choir Robe Company in Dallas and then dress it up with some decoration. The fellows even insisted on teaching me the secret Armadillo sign, which was nothing more than making a fist, but leaving the thumb and little finger sticking out on either end. From there, the little finger is tucked behind the ear, leaving the thumb pointing out behind the head. The thumb is then wiggled up and down, supposedly like an armadillo tail waving.

I was standing there, watching a barn full of grown men doing this, and it was genuinely hard to keep from bursting out laughing. I worked hard and gathered my composure. Finally, I gave my critique. "You know, fellows, most secret signs are supposed to look natural. That way the general public doesn't catch onto it."

There were puzzled expressions all over the room. Skeeter finally stepped up and said, "Yeah," kind of questioningly.

I gave them a sympathetic smile. "Well, at a glance, the Armadillo symbol kind of looks like someone cleaning out his ear with his little finger."

Heads nodded all around. "Yep," Skeeter smiled, "that was exactly what we were going for!"

I just started nodding my head with them, forcing a grin. Right at that moment, I knew I was going to have to avoid giving the secret Armadillo sign at all cost.

Initiation Pepper Wings

20 chicken wings
1 stick of butter
½ cup olive oil
½ cup lemon juice
6 large garlic cloves, crushed
1 Tbsp red pepper
1 tsp salt

1 tsp ground white pepper
1 tsp ground black pepper
a few cans of beer

Put the wings in a pot, and pour enough beer in to cover them. Put the pot on the stove, and bring the beer to a boil. Reduce the heat, and let the wings simmer for 15 minutes.

While those are cooking, preheat the oven to 375 degrees and mix all the other ingredients together in a bowl. It's helpful to melt the butter in the microwave first. After the wings are done, discard the beer, and coat each wing in the pepper sauce. Put them on a greased, shallow pan and bake for 15 to 20 minutes. After you take them out, lightly sprinkle with black pepper to taste. If you'd prefer them to be a little more spicy, add some red pepper as well.

Fiery Lemon Wings

20 chicken wings
½ cup lemon juice
1 cup of your favorite hot sauce
1 tsp cayenne pepper
1 tsp white pepper
1 tsp garlic powder
1 Tbsp paprika
1 Tbsp butter

Start by preheating the oven to 375 degrees. While you're waiting for it to come up to temperature, heat the butter in the microwave until it is soft. Spray a cookie sheet with a vegetable spray, and you're ready to get started.

Combine the softened butter, lemon juice, hot sauce, and spices together in a bowl. Dip each wing in the mixture, coating them, then place on the cookie sheet. Bake them in the oven for about 15 minutes, then remove the pan. Brush each wing with the mixture, both sides, then bake for another 15 minutes. Repeat the above process one more time, then cook them until the wings are done—at least a final 15 minutes.

Rosemary Wings

20 chicken wings
⅓ cup finely chopped fresh rosemary
⅓ cup cooking oil
½ cup dry white wine
¼ tsp white pepper
¼-½ tsp salt
½ tsp black pepper
2 Tbsp minced green onion

Mix all of the ingredients together in a bowl to form a marinade, add the chicken wings, and put them in the refrigerator overnight. Be sure to save the marinade when you take them out.

You can cook these in the oven or over a grill, but in either case brush them with the marinade about every 10 minutes. In the oven, you'll be cooking them for about 45 minutes at 375 degrees. The grilling time will vary, depending on how hot your coals are. In either case, these are going to be great!

The Wrath of Irma

I put aside worrying about the duty of procuring my armadillo hat for the time being and after a few days decided to go down to the local dirt track and watch the stock cars race. I loved watching the big boys race on television, but there was nothing quite like being there live at one of the rural oval tracks.

This one was about twenty miles away and drew drivers from all over the county. Some of them were hoping to make it to the big time, others wanted to raise a little money just to keep their race cars running, and a few were only there to have a wild time out there in the fray. Whatever their reasons, those racers put their heart and soul into their driving.

I paid my ten bucks at the gate, then took a seat up in the grandstands. Even though there was a pretty good crowd, I didn't see anyone I recognized yet, so I just sat there and waited for the first race to begin.

I wasn't paying a lot of attention as the drivers were taking their practice laps, and since I was at the event solo, I figured the best time to hit the concession stand was before everything got started. I had to walk past the pit area to get there, since they were butted right up against the front of the grandstands. The scent of gasoline and burned rubber started mingling with the odor of greasy fries and popcorn from the stand, but suddenly, somewhere in between the two, I caught the unmistakable whiff of my uncle's honey-mustard wings.

That was impossible, of course. I knew for a fact that Uncle Bubba was helping Buck build an addition to his smokehouse. He'd told me so that very morning. I questioned why Buck needed more room in his smokehouse, since it was larger than most people's kitchens, but when it came to Buck and curing meat you just never knew.

I stopped and smelled the air again and was certain. Perhaps Uncle Bubba had prepared a batch for someone. In fact, if he ever did get that restaurant open, I'd have to get used to smelling his wonderful varieties all over the area. He wasn't quite there yet, though, so I decided to check it out.

I walked back along the fence that separated the pits from the grandstand. Everything looked normal. Each pit contained a few toolboxes that belonged to the driver or the mechanics. In most, an extra set of tires rested near the simple wooden bench that served more as a table than a seat for the crew. The cars had already moved out onto the track and were making their slow prerace circles.

Since the crews had been working hard to get their cars ready, they were now taking a short break. I passed stall after stall in the pits, and about halfway down I stopped dead in my tracks. Sitting there on a bench, in a stall that had the number 23 hanging on the fence behind it, sat Skeeter and Buck. My stomach turned over in my belly.

The fence was only a four-footer, so I climbed over it without much effort. I was able to walk up on them without either one seeing me first. "'Evening, Buck. Skeeter." Their eyes got as wide as moon pies.

"Uh," Skeeter hesitated, "your uncle's not here." I don't think I'd heard a lie that bad since elementary school.

"Is that right, Buck?" I asked. He just sat there staring at me, holding a wing in his hand. I could only guess what was really going on. "Fellows, what has my uncle got you involved in now?"

They didn't have to answer, because right about that time Uncle Bubba roared by on the track. He was driving Aunt Irma's 1989 blue Ford LTD, and there was a big white 23 painted on the door. Through the open side window I could hear him yell, "Yeeeeee-haaawwww!!!"

I stood there dumbfounded. After a minute, I turned back to Skeeter and Buck, who were sitting on the bench like two kids in the principal's office. "Exactly what does Uncle Bubba think he's doing?"

Buck finally said, "He's entering one of the stock car races tonight." He shrugged. "The prize is five hundred dollars, and he figured that would help get his chicken wing restaurant started."

I couldn't believe what I was hearing. "But guys, he's never driven in a single race in his life! These folks do this every week!" I just shook my head. "Can you imagine what Aunt Irma is going to do to him when she finds out? Good Lord, boys, he's even painted a number on the side of her car!"

"Just shoe polish," Skeeter offered.

Clearly, Uncle Bubba had lost his mind. This was the craziest thing that I'd seen him do in I don't know how long. At least Aunt Irma would be spared watching this certain fiasco.

Or so I thought.

Aunt Irma had never attended a stock car race in her life. That's why it was so surprising to look up into the stands and see her sitting there next to Mrs. Oralee Franklin. My knees felt weak, and there was a sick feeling in my gut. I quickly looked down at Skeeter and Buck. "If there is any way you two can get Uncle Bubba off that dirt track, you do it!" I demanded. With that, I hopped the fence and worked my way through the grandstand crowd to Aunt Irma.

She jumped up and gave me a big hug when I got there. "Why, Nephew, isn't this exciting!"

I wondered just what was going on. Surely she wasn't a party to it all. "Why, course it is, Aunt Irma. But I didn't know that you like the races."

She smiled like she was a country girl who'd gone to the big city for the first time. "Oh, hon, I just came out here with Oralee to watch her boy race. I've never seen anything like this in my life, though. Just look how fast they're going out there!"

While I'd been fretting over the whole situation, the race had begun in earnest. The spectators had all jumped to their feet and were whooping and hollering in a deafening roar. Aunt Irma was standing up on her tiptoes trying to see over the crowd, and under different circumstances I would have really gotten a kick out of the thrilled expression on her face.

Her smile suddenly froze, and her eyes began to slowly widen. "Oh, no," she said in a soft voice. "That's Bubba out there."

Her eyes instantly narrowed and her brow furrowed. "And that's my car he's driving!" There was no hiding her rage as she began pushing her way through the crowd and down toward the pits. "Bubba!" she was yelling the whole time. "You get my car off that track right this instant!"

I'd always heard that in times of stress, ordinary humans can do things that would normally be impossible, and now I believe it. Aunt Irma hopped the fence with an agility that I could only wish for.

She headed right for Skeeter and Buck. When they looked up and saw her coming, those fellows bolted in opposite directions. I guess neither of them wanted to confront the wrath of Irma.

Unfortunately, Skeeter was a little slow getting away and my aunt grabbed him by his ear, holding him in place while he yelped. I remembered that my first grade teacher used to do the same thing as she dragged one of us to the coatroom for a whipping.

"Skeeter," she hissed at him. "You get this race stopped right now, before Bubba hurts himself or my car. Are you listening to me?" She gave his head a little shake using his ear as a handle.

"Ow, Irma, come on now." His face was twisted up in an expression of pain. "Besides, it was Bubba's idea!"

"Then you just help me get Bubba off that track." Her tone of voice was as stern as her expression. "I mean it, Skeeter."

He hummed and hawed, but finally acquiesced. "Ouch! Okay, okay, let's head over to the starting line. I'll see what I can do."

Aunt Irma walked along in front of the pit stalls with her arm outstretched, leading Skeeter by the ear. I followed a few steps behind them. The other pit crews were whooping and hollering and pointing at Skeeter. If my aunt's hold on his ear hadn't hurt so bad, he might have been embarrassed.

"Buck!" Skeeter yelled suddenly, and I followed his gaze over to the parking lot. I saw the pickup with the rack of horns mounted on front cruising along the edge of the lot, and I figured Buck was giving a quick pass to see if there was anything he could do for his friend. He must have realized that in the great scheme of things, sometimes sacrifices have to be made, because the truck spun dirt and gravel for yards behind it, then roared out onto the highway. He quickly disappeared into the night—Buck must have been doing ninety when he hit the pavement.

We were almost to the flag stand, and Aunt Irma gave Skeeter a tug to get him back in motion. When we got there, she finally released him. Skeeter cupped his ear like he was going to protect it from the world at all cost. He glared at my aunt. "Damn, Irma, you hurt me!"

She hit him square in the back of his head with her purse. "You hold that vile tongue around me, Skeeter!" He recoiled with his arms around his head, and she popped him once again. "My husband may allow that kind of language in his presence, but I am a lady and expect to be treated as such!"

Of course, I knew that Bubba not only allowed such language, but probably encouraged it. This just didn't seem like it was the time to interject such a thought.

Skeeter eased his way over to the flag stand's ladder, being very careful not to turn his back on my aunt. He carefully climbed about halfway up to the small stand where the flagman oversaw the race and motioned for the official to come down.

In only a moment Skeeter was on the ground beside me and the race official was stepping down off the ladder.

The young man looked flustered. He puffed viciously on a cigarette that was hanging from the side of his mouth and looked from one of us to the other like he was trying to decide who had called him away from his duties. He pushed up the bill of his gimmie cap and waited for an explanation.

Aunt Irma raised her chin up. "Are you the fellow in charge of this thing?"

He nodded his head. "Yes ma'am, I'm the track official here. In fact, since Jimmy Ray didn't show up, I'm the only one." He crossed his arms, smoke still billowing from the cigarette. "Just what's so all-fired important that you had to get me down in the middle of a race?"

"My husband is driving my car in this race, and I want it stopped right this moment." She stared at him, and raised one eyebrow. "Do I make myself clear, sir?"

He just chuckled. "I'm awful sorry, but this race has a few more laps to go. There's no way I can stop it now, even if I wanted to."

Aunt Irma studied him for a moment. "You sure do look familiar. Aren't you Minnie Mae Jensen's boy?"

I watched as his authoritative demeanor melted before my very eyes. "Y-yes ma'am. She's my mom."

"Does your mother know you're here, son?" She eyed him suspiciously.

As the cars continued to roar by, he just stood there stammering. "Well, I mean, of course she knows I'm here, ma'am." He quickly removed his cap and held it respectfully down at his side.

Aunt Irma reached up and snatched the cigarette from his mouth, threw it on the gravel, and ground it out with the heel of her shoe. "I've a good mind to tell your dear, sweet mother what her son's doing, holding a race and smoking cigarettes."

"But, ma'am, I'm twenty-one, and my mother," he started.

"Your mother would be heartbroken to see her son like this!" she interrupted. "Parading around in front of this crowd with a cigarette hanging out of your face. What kind of example is that for your younger sister?"

He raised his hands to my aunt, palms open as if to calm her down. "Okay, ma'am, just tell me what you want from me."

My aunt looked him square in the eyes. "You climb up on your platform there and end this race this very instant."

He hesitated for a moment, then shimmied up the ladder. These dirt track races were unpredictable, and usually unorganized, in small rural areas like ours. There might be some grumbling about the race stopping prematurely, but most everyone would be gearing up for the second race of the night, where the prize money was even better than the five hundred that the winner of this race would get.

I watched as the fellow waved the white flag, letting everyone know that the final lap had arrived. I scanned the track looking for Uncle Bubba. I wanted to make sure he was still in one piece. I suddenly got the biggest surprise of my life: My uncle was leading the race!

They came back around, and Uncle Bubba was squeezing more out of that car than Aunt Irma had ever thought about. It had probably been saving all that pent-up energy in its metal innards all these years, just waiting for the chance to use it.

When the cars came back around he was still in the lead. The black-and-white checkered flag waved high in the air as my uncle crossed the finish line, giving another "Yeeeeee-haaawwww!!!" to the crowd.

He wheeled Aunt Irma's blue Ford off the track and into the winner's circle. We all ran over there to greet him, and when my aunt got there she threw her arms around him and gave him the biggest hug I'd ever seen. She patted his arms, like she was checking to see if he was really okay.

Bubba just grinned. "Welcome to victory lane, dear!" The track official who had helped Aunt Irma by ending the race stepped up and handed my uncle a check. I caught a glimpse of it and saw that it was indeed for the full five hundred dollars that Skeeter and Buck had mentioned earlier.

He beamed and held the check up for all to see. For a moment, anyway. Aunt Irma snatched it out of his hand and tucked it quickly out of sight. "I'll take that money to do any repairs to my car, Bubba."

He looked hurt, like she had taken his victory away. "But Irma," he pleaded.

"But nothing!" She had an angry set to her face once again, now that she was certain that he was all right. "You and Skeeter take my LTD to the car wash immediately, do you understand me? I want it to be spotless before you bring it home!"

"But Irma," he said again, but she quickly silenced him with a glance that would set slow-dry concrete. He recoiled, and Skeeter quickly ducked behind him. "Of course, dear, we'll get right on it."

By that time, Mrs. Oralee Franklin had made her way over to Aunt Irma, and they glared at Uncle Bubba in unison, then disappeared into the crowd.

Bubba was walking back over to the car when he saw me standing there. "Nephew! Did you see me win the race?"

I couldn't help but smile. "Sure did, Uncle Bubba. I found your pit right as the race was getting started."

His brow crinkled. "But you couldn't have known that I entered the race—how'd you find it?"

I smiled again. "The wings, Uncle, the wings."

He raised an eyebrow, nodded his approval at my answer, and climbed behind the wheel of the LTD. He only hesitated a second before driving away, and I figured he was looking for any excuse to delay facing Aunt Irma again. I'm sure that all the way home he was rehearsing the announcement of his retirement from stock car racing.

Honey-Mustard Wings

20 chicken wings
1 cup plain yogurt
½ cup honey
⅓ cup Dijon mustard
2 Tbsp dark brown sugar
1 Tbsp soy sauce
1 Tbsp olive oil
¼ cup minced shallots
1 Tbsp thyme

Preheat your oven to 375 degrees, and coat a casserole dish with any non-stick vegetable spray. Combine all the other ingredients in another bowl, and coat each wing with the mixture. Place the wings in the dish and cover with foil and then bake them for 45 minutes.

Next, remove the foil and use any extra coating to brush on the wings, and continue baking, uncovered, for another 10 minutes or until the chicken is done. I'm sure the wings are going to taste much better in your kitchen than they did when Skeeter and Buck were mingling them with all that smoke and dirt from the track!

12

Cut Plug Friday the Thirteenth

Jgot a call from my uncle about a week after he and Skeeter had been forced to scrub Aunt Irma's Ford clean. He wanted me to meet him in town at the square, and although I had no idea why, I figured that it would at least kill a Friday evening.

When I arrived, he was standing beside his pickup holding a plastic ice chest in one hand and a rope in the other. Before I could ask what was going on, he had turned away and headed across the square toward Arnold Underwood's Hardware store. "C'mon, Nephew!" He was walking at a pretty good clip, like he was a man on a mission.

We circled around behind the store where there was a ladder leaning up against the building. Uncle Bubba stopped long enough to tie one end of the rope to the handle of the cooler. Once it was secured, he grabbed the other end and started up the ladder.

I just stood there on the ground, staring up at my uncle's rump ascending into the heavens. At least as far as the roof of the hardware store, anyway. "Uncle Bubba, what in the world are you doing?"

"Just climb on up here. It's the best seat in the house." He stepped onto the roof, then swung his other leg off the ladder.

I stepped onto the first rung with more than a little apprehension. "Uncle Bubba, does Mr. Underwood know that you're getting up onto his roof?"

"Just come on, Nephew." He leaned over the top and motioned for me to join him, then proceeded to pull up the ice chest. I looked around and since we seemed to be alone, started to climb.

My uncle had taken a position over at one of the back corners, not far away from the ladder. This gave me a little bit of comfort—just in case we had to make a fast getaway.

I looked around and found a wooden crate similar to the one he was sitting on. It wasn't hard to spot one. People crammed on top of the town square buildings on the rare occasions that Cut Plug got to actually have a parade, and more than one person had apparently left their make-shift seats up here for the next event.

As I pulled my seat beside his, Uncle Bubba opened up the cooler and produced a couple of colas. Mine was a little warm, and when I questioned it Bubba just smiled.

"I brought us some wings to watch all the excitement!" He pulled out a foil package, and when he unwrapped it the most wonderful smell of ginger filled our little corner of the roof. He followed it with a second foil bundle, and from it I caught a whiff of lemon and garlic blending together.

I grabbed one of the ginger wings and quickly bit into it, all the while wondering what the excitement might be. It wasn't a holiday. It actually was Friday the thirteenth, but that wasn't anything to celebrate.

Uncle Bubba was quiet, so I thought I'd throw something out. "Well, Aunt Irma caught me after church last Sunday to get me to look at her car. I noticed that you could still see a ghost of the number *23* on its side where the shoe polish must have soaked into the old layer of paint." I paused to take a bite of the wing, enjoying the wonderful ginger flavor, when my uncle looked over at me like he was worried about what I'd said. "Course, I didn't let on like I did. I just carried on about how good it looked."

He laughed for a second. "I 'preciate that, Nephew. I really do. That whole thing was just an example of how screwed up I've gotten things."

There was something in his voice that sounded kind of sad. "What are you talking about, Uncle Bubba?"

He finished chewing the meat off the lemon-garlic wing in his hand and threw the bone into the cooler. "I don't know,

Nephew, it's like I can't do anything right these days." He sighed heavily. "I mean, I want to open the chicken wing restaurant more than anything else in the world. Trickle wouldn't lend me the money, and none of those credit card companies came through. I thought I might at least have a start when I won the money from the race. Irma was so mad that I might've banged up her car a little, she took the money for damages. I just can't catch a break on this thing." His head dropped a little. "Maybe I should just be content to stay at the cement plant. It's a good job; I've got a wonderful wife and a nice home. Who could want anything more than that?"

I felt really bad. If I had even one spare dollar I would have given it to my uncle right then and there.

"Yep," he continued, "I just can't figure it out. I can pull off the most intricate plan when it comes to a practical joke, but when it's something serious like my wing restaurant, I can't make it happen."

As sympathetic as I felt toward him, a few things suddenly clicked together in my mind: roof, Friday the thirteenth, intricate plan, and practical joke. "Uh, Uncle Bubba, I'm thinking that I ought to know what we're doing up here on the roof of the hardware store."

Bubba picked up another wing, took a bite, and nodded over across the alley. Even with a mouthful of chicken, he said, "Look one street over. The big white house on the corner."

"Yeah." I shrugged. "Mr. Trickle's house."

"Well I figured I owed Patterson a good one. After all, when Skeeter, Buck, and me saw that UFO, that rascal Patterson didn't believe us and even pulled that trick on me with his truck a few days later." He chuckled, a huge smile on his face. "Well paybacks from Bubba don't always come right away. Besides, I figured I'd go for a twofer and get Trickle a little as well."

I got that feeling in the pit of my stomach again. "Uncle Bubba, what have you done?"

If it was possible, his grin got even bigger. "I'm telling you, Nephew, this one is a work of art. I started it two weeks ago. Irma and me were eating supper, when I told her that Mr. Patterson had applied for a home improvement loan over at the bank and had been turned down."

I had a bad feeling about this. "Had he?"

"Course not!" Uncle Bubba frowned, like I should have realized that the story was only part of his master plan. "Irma didn't know that, though. So I told her that he was holding Trickle personally responsible."

I was still a little confused. "But he didn't really apply."

"Not even! Now pay attention, Nephew, it just gets more convoluted from here, so you've gotta stay with me. Anyway, a couple of days later I mentioned it again. I told her that Mr. Patterson had been bragging out at the plant how he was going to get even with Trickle and show him a thing or two. I told her there was something in the tone of his voice that made the hair on the back of my neck stand up." He stopped for a second to finish off the wing in his hand. "I also reminded her that Mr. Patterson had done all that time in the mental hospital several decades back." Bubba's eyes narrowed, and his voice dropped to a whisper. "Rumor has it that he was committed for all those terrible killings over in Arkansas, where some poor folks were cut up with a chain saw." He was nodding his head slowly.

"Uncle Bubba, what have you done?" I couldn't believe what I was hearing. "Mr. Patterson's never been in a mental home!"

He cackled and slapped his knee. "Well of course! Irma said the same thing, but I just told her that it'd been hushed up so as not to scare the townsfolk. The chain saw killer story just sounded like such a scandal that I knew she wouldn't be able to resist telling the tale at the Garden Club meeting last weekend."

I closed my eyes and shook my head. "Oh man, Uncle Bubba. I'm not too sure about this."

76

"Nonsense. It's going to be great. Anyway, a couple of evenings this week I sneaked out in the middle of the night and drove over to Trickle's house and cranked up my chain saw right under his window. As soon as the light snapped on, I beat it back to the house as fast as I could. I figured it probably scared the bejeebers out of that tight old fellow. I was just getting warmed up, though."

I sat there listening to my uncle and staring at Trickle's house, wondering exactly what he had in store. It just couldn't be good.

"You see, Nephew, the most important thing to understand in a small town like Cut Plug is that everyone loves to spread gossip. There's just no doubt in my mind that Irma filled the Garden Club with horror stories about Mr. Patterson. I'm sure Marianne Trickle carried those stories straight home to her husband, too." He took a small break to down another wing, all the while watching the banker's house. "Anyway, my big plan comes together tonight." The sun was just setting enough that we could see that the lights were on in the Trickles' house. "Look, he's already home."

It wasn't the suspense that was getting to me—it was the uneasy feeling in my stomach. "Okay, Uncle Bubba. Spill. What in the world's going on here?"

He beamed again. "Well, Nephew, this one's going to be the prank to end all pranks. It took a little planning, mind you, but it's all going to be worth it." He pointed over to the Trickle's house. "Now the first challenge was to make sure that the old banker was home alone."

I had to interrupt. "Wait a minute. The Queen of Hearts Bridge Club meet on Fridays, and isn't this the evening they play the Lady Aces Club from Tater Springs?" Tater Springs was a town only slightly larger than Cut Plug, and being only twenty miles away, it was our rival in everything from high school football to the annual tournament between the towns' bridge clubs. Since Aunt Irma was a member, I had a sudden fear that she was accidentally going to be dragged into the middle of Uncle Bubba's plan.

Bubba nodded his head. "Oh, that one was an obstacle, all right. But then I remembered that they alternated playing at the club presidents' houses. They played here in Cut Plug last year at Marianne Trickle's house, since she's the president and all. This year they have to be playing in Tater Springs."

I sensed trouble. "Uh, Uncle Bubba, did you check with Aunt Irma on that?"

"Of course not! I didn't want to get her suspicions up."

I had started to say something else, but Bubba held up his hand.

"Shhhh, not now." He put his finger to his lips. "Just watch!" He pointed down below us, and I saw a figure running from the hardware store. I was caught off guard and leapt to my feet—the man was carrying a chain saw and wearing a hockey mask.

"Nephew, sit down!" he said, pulling me back to my crate. "It just gets better from here."

I'd had enough. "Uncle Bubba, I've just gotta insist that you fill me in on this scheme of yours! Now, out with it!"

"You're not going to believe it." My uncle giggled. He honestly giggled like a schoolboy. "See, once I was sure that the ladies were going to be out of the house, I knew that Trickle would be there alone. I also knew for certain that Mr. Patterson would stop by the hardware store for coffee about this time like he does every Friday night. He and Mr. Underwood are pretty tight, them being in the Korean War together and all. They've had coffee here every Friday night for the last hundred years. Hell, it's why Underwood even keeps the store open on Friday evenings."

I had to interrupt him. "But who's that fellow with the chain saw, and where's he going?"

Uncle Bubba held up his hand. "Just hang on now, I'm getting to that. A little while ago I stopped by the hardware store and started asking Mr. Underwood for stuff that he had to go digging in the back for. While he was doing that, I hid all the welding masks, safety goggles, and every other face protection that I could find."

"You don't mean you were shoplifting that stuff out of there." I knew my uncle was honest, but he seemed to be a little too involved in this plan for his own good.

"No, of course not!" He grimaced. "No way I'd do something like that—I just kind of put them out of sight. When he came back out front, I showed him the hockey mask that I'd brought in with me. I told Mr. Underwood that a lot of the kids were getting into street hockey, and he'd probably make a few dollars if he started stocking things like that. I casually left it on the counter for him to study on. Sure enough, as I left, Mr. Patterson was coming in."

As Uncle Bubba spun his tale, I watched the masked figure crossing the field behind the hardware store. It was pretty clear that he was heading straight for the Trickle's house.

Uncle Bubba tapped me on the knee. "Listen up, now! You've gotta hear the whole thing before the action starts. So anyway, on the way out of the store I stopped Patterson and asked what he was doing there, since the Volunteer Fire Department was doing some practicing by burning down Edwardson's old chicken coop. I told him that everyone was going to be there. Of course, I figured he'd pass that info onto Mr. Underwood. Since Underwood is such a rabid member of the Fire Department, I knew beyond a shadow of a doubt that he'd beat feet right over there to join his buddies."

I was starting to understand. "But there's really no fire practice, is there, Uncle Bubba?"

"Course not. But just like I planned, Underwood left Mr. Patterson in charge of the store. Right before you showed up I called the store and made my voice gruff, just like Underwood's, to fool Patterson into thinking it was him. I said the Volunteer Fire Department had just gotten a call that Mr. Trickle was doing some remodeling and a wall fell down on him in his wife's new sewing room. I went on and on about how he needed some help real fast. I told him to grab a chain saw, fill it with oil and gas, then head right over to Trickle's house and cut the banker out from under the wall before it crushed him completely. I warned him, though, to wear some kind of face protection since the splinters would be flying everywhere." He rared back, full of pride. "So banker Trickle's going to get a little surprise. What do you think of my plan?"

The masked figure that I now knew was Mr. Patterson was almost to the house. "Uncle Bubba, I see a couple of problems here. First of all, I think your memory's a little fuzzy on the big bridge tournament. I know for sure they had it over in Tater Springs last year, because the ladies borrowed the church van and I drove them over there."

He stopped grinning, and a worried looked locked onto his face. "You did? Are you sure about that, Nephew?"

"Positive. I had to sit there while all those women played out their tournament, slinging tales and gossiping the whole time."

Bubba stood up. "I can't believe it, Nephew. Then how could the Queen of Hearts Bridge Club have decided to get out of the house?"

This was news that my uncle wasn't going to enjoy hearing. "As far as I know, they haven't. The Trickles have that big driveway with the basketball goal out behind their house, so the ladies are all probably parked back there. I'm sure that they and the women from the Tater Springs Lady Aces are a good ways into the first game."

"And Mr. Trickle?" His face had taken on a pallor of horror, realizing that Aunt Irma was in the house.

"At the bank. It's been closed all day, since the auditors are in town. They've had signs up for the last week. All the lights were still on when I first got here."

I saw true terror on his face. "Oh, Lord. So Patterson's going to storm into the middle of the bridge club's tournament waving that chain saw and wearing that hockey mask?"

I shrugged. "Afraid so, Uncle Bubba."

He sat down hard on his crate. "Irma's going to kill me, Nephew. She's going to kill me graveyard dead."

It was probably true. We watched in silence as the masked Patterson yanked the cord of his chain saw and then threw open the door of Trickle's house. He charged inside to a chorus of screams that could be heard even from the rooftop of Underwood's Hardware Store.

Although he had only been inside for a minute or less, it seemed like an eternity. The screams had subsided and blended into a single yell. The source became apparent as the masked figure burst forth from the front door of the house, one arm flailing wildly and the other dragging a chain saw that had been switched off somewhere in the course of matters. Following close at his heels was the entire roster of the Queen of Hearts Bridge Club and the Lady Aces. Marianne Trickle was leading the pack, with my Aunt Irma running a close second. They were yelling and screaming and throwing things at him. Mr. Patterson was clearly in trouble.

I suppose desperation fuels the fire in people, because Mr. Patterson was moving like a diesel truck with the pedal down. He began to put more and more distance between himself and the ladies, until it was finally apparent that he was going to make a clean getaway.

Uncle Bubba sat there dumbfounded. Slowly, deliberately, his lips began to form words. "Uh-oh," was all he said.

I stopped to reflect for a minute. "You know, Uncle Bubba, if you were to get in your truck and go rescue Mr. Patterson, then get him back to the hardware store before Mr. Underwood returns or the ladies see you, everything might just be okay. You'd have to tell him the whole story, but once you're back you could both tell everyone that you'd been talking in the store all evening."

He shot me a worried glance. "But what about the story I told about the Volunteer Fire Department?"

It was my turn to smile. "Just a bit of bad information—but Underwood will probably be coming back any minute."

"And the chainsaw maniac would remain a mystery," Uncle Bubba added. A glimmer of hope shown in his eyes. "Nephew, I hate to ditch you like this, but I've gotta go." He ran the few steps to the ladder, then shimmied down it faster than I've ever seen him move. He disappeared around the store, on his way to extract Mr. Patterson from danger.

As for me, I sat there on the roof for another full hour, doing my best to finish those fantastic wings, and watching the aftermath. Cut Plug's never had a serial killer before, so the town was primed for hot gossip about one. I don't think I'll ever eat those wings again without being reminded of that particular Friday the thirteenth.

I know it won't be the same, but you can still try the wing recipes we had that evening. I'll never forget munching on them up on Underwood's Hardware Store roof, overlooking the town of Cut Plug. Without a good ladder, though, I'd recommend that you enjoy the wings in the comfort of your own home.

Ginger Wings

20 chicken wings
¼ cup dark corn syrup
¼ cup soy sauce
4 Tbsp honey
4 Tbsp lemon juice
½ cup chicken broth mixed with 1 Tbsp cornstarch
¼ lb. mushrooms, chopped
2 green onions, sliced
1 Tbsp olive oil
2 tsp minced fresh ginger
2 Tbsp dry sherry

Mix the corn syrup, soy sauce, honey, and lemon juice in a large bowl, then add the chicken wings. Uncle Bubba marinates the wings for a couple of hours at room temperature, but to be safe, I'd do it in the refrigerator. Then remove the wings, reserving the marinade.

In your favorite skillet, heat the olive oil over medium-high heat. Put in the chicken wings and the ginger. You'll want to stir these around for 5 to 10 minutes. After that you can stir in the marinade and the cooking sherry. Add the mushrooms and green onions next, stirring frequently for about 5 minutes. Add the chicken broth and cornstarch mixture next, and bring the entire mixture to a boil. Reduce the heat; cover, and simmer for about 20 minutes or until the wings are tender. Take them out of the mixture and serve on a platter.

Garlicky Lemon Pepper Wings

20 chicken wings
½ cup lemon juice
2 Tbsp garlic powder
1 Tbsp black pepper
1 tsp salt
1 tsp paprika
1 tsp salt
¼ cup olive oil

Begin by mixing all ingredients in a bowl, and marinate the wings in the refrigerator overnight. Save the marinade. Preheat the oven to 375 degrees, then bake the wings for 15 minutes on a cookie sheet that's been coated with vegetable spray. Rotate each wing, brushing with the marinade, and cook for another 20 to 30 minutes. Discard any remaining marinade.

Secret Emergency Armadillo Meeting

I didn't know what was going on that Saturday morning, but there was something that everyone seemed to know about but me. Early in the day I stopped to gas up my truck, and as I was pumping the last few gallons, Mr. Trembley pulled up at the pump beside me in his big double-cab pickup. Even though I've worked within spitting distance from him at the plant for I don't know how many years, he ignored me like I wasn't even there. As I was putting the gas cap back on, I looked over and noticed that he had made a fist and tucked his little finger behind his ear. His thumb was pointing backwards, swinging up and down like he was cleaning out his ear something fierce. Mr. Trembley was giving the sign of the Armadillo.

I looked around—thankfully, we were pretty much alone. I just nodded and smiled, then got out of there as fast as possible. My next stop was at Hinkley's Grocery, and as I was innocently pushing my shopping cart though the short, narrow aisles of Cut Plug's only food store, I happened to look up and see Elmer Schlackman back behind the butcher counter. Elmer had been cutting meat for years, and I'd bought every single ounce of steak and hamburger that had ever touched my grill from him. I smiled and nodded a greeting, but Elmer just turned the other way. He kind of glanced around, then carefully made the waggling motion; it was another Armadillo sign.

I didn't know what was happening, but I knew who would. I checked out as fast as I could and steered my truck over to Uncle Bubba's house.

When I rolled into the driveway, he was walking from the garage over to the house. "Uncle Bubba!" I yelled through my open widow.

He hurried around to my side of the cab. "Nephew! I'm awful glad to see you—I've been trying to catch up with you all day!" He narrowed his eyes and carefully surveyed the area, then leaned in toward me. In a whisper, he said, "There's a top secret emergency meeting of the Armadillos tonight."

Apparently the Loyal Order was taking it much more seriously than I was. I just sighed. "Okay, Uncle, I'll bite. What's going on?"

He shook his head. "Dunno. All I know is that I got a call from an Armadillo who said this was a critical point in the history of our lodge. He said he'd fill me in with everyone else at the meeting."

I still wasn't sure about this whole Armadillo thing, but until I was able to get a handle on it, I was going to play along. "Okay, Uncle Bubba. What time?"

He glanced carefully around again. "Eight o'clock. And don't forget to bring something for the pot-luck."

"The Armadillos are going to have a pot-luck supper, even at an emergency meeting?" I just had to wonder about these fellows.

My uncle looked like he almost took offense at my question. "Course, Nephew. The main thing about the lodge is the fellowship with your brother Armadillos."

After only a few seconds of thought, I determined that a tub of mustard potato salad from the local grocery would allow me to commune with them just fine. "Fair enough. I'll see you there." Uncle Bubba just nodded, and I pulled out of the driveway and headed back home.

A few hours later, I drove over to Junior Newton's barn where the brethren were gathering. I was still the only one without a hat and a robe, so I stood out like an atheist at a revival meeting. I guess it was still so close to my induction that no one seemed to care, though. I kind of hung to myself over to one side. I was a little creeped out by the prospect of having a conversation with anyone wearing a dead armadillo on their head. As much as I tried not to, my gaze kept going up to those beady little black eyes staring down at me. It gave me the willies.

The buzz among the Armadillo members was intense, with everyone wondering exactly what the emergency was all about. When everyone was finally assembled, Uncle Bubba took his place behind a pedestal with an armadillo painted on it. He banged the gavel and silence slowly crept over the Armadillos.

"Brothers," he started, "I have been told that there is a grave situation facing the lodge. While I don't know any of the details, Brother Armadillo Abernathy is going to fill us all in on the situation." He stepped aside, and Mr. Abernathy took the position behind the pedestal.

"Fellow Armadillos, a challenge is facing our lodge." He paused to let that sink in, and there were more than a few whispers around the room. "I have it on very good authority that tomorrow the mayor will announce a Fourth of July parade for next week."

Uncle Bubba was the first to speak. "How in the world can that be? I thought Anester, that old horse's butt, was keeping any parades off of our streets."

"There's always been a homecoming parade," one fellow in the back offered.

My uncle swelled up. "Of course there is! Hell, Anester's daughter has been in the homecoming court for the last three years. God forbid that she serves in the military during wartime, but I bet we'd get a Memorial Day parade out of that deal."

Buck stood. "So how do you know about all this?"

Mr. Abernathy held his hand up. "I'm getting to that part. You all know that my wife and Anester's wife both teach over at the junior high, and their rooms are right next to each other. Well Anester's wife let it slip that she got her husband to approve a parade so she could bring that fact to the garden club. With news like that, she was hoping they'd let her join."

It was Skeeter who took the floor next. "So what does that have to do with the Fourth of July?" he asked, looking puzzled.

"It has everything to do with it!" Abernathy's brow wrinkled. "The ladies from the garden club will be chigger-itchin' to build a float made of flowers just like they do in some of those big-city parades. The thing is, the Loyal Order of the Armadillo won't be represented if we don't take steps immediately! I propose that we begin planning a float right away!"

There were murmurs and nods of approval all around the barn. I finally had to speak up. "Excuse me, fellows but aren't we supposed to be a secret order? How can we have a float in a parade?"

Everyone just stared at me with blank expressions, but one by one they slowly turned to scowls. I guess it is much more fun to have a float in a parade than to be a secret lodge. I was outvoted by their glances alone.

Uncle Bubba took a position behind the podium once again and cleared his throat. "Uh, I guess there is something to what my nephew's sayin'. We're gonna have to figure out something that represents the lodge without giving away any of our secrets. I recommend that we appoint a committee," he went on, "for which we'll take nominations from the floor."

"Buck!" a voice boomed out, and my uncle banged his gavel in acceptance. "Abernathy!" another called. The gavel sounded again. "Skeeter!" rang out, from a voice that sounded suspiciously like Skeeter himself, but Uncle Bubba pounded the podium to accept it nonetheless.

"As Grand Dillo, I'll head up the committee myself. Now, is there any other business, or can we call this emergency meeting closed and dig in?"

I'd almost forgotten about the pot-luck. On the way over I'd stopped by Hinkley's Grocery and picked up a couple of tubs of the wonderful mustard potato salad that his wife made fresh every morning. They had been sitting on the seat of my pickup, so as my uncle banged the gavel and the members began to mill around, I took the opportunity to duck outside for my contribution to the pot-luck dinner.

Once I'd returned, I saw that Junior had set up a few card tables in the back of the barn, presumably for the food. I carried my potato salad over and took a quick inventory. On one table was a big aluminum pan that contained a heaping pile of chicken wings. I recognized them immediately, of course, as Uncle

Bubba's Mexican fajita wings. The other two tables were filled with paper bags where the Armadillos hadn't taken out their pot-luck entrees yet.

Uncle Bubba suddenly appeared at my side and slapped me on the back. "Well, Nephew, if you'll give me a hand this'll go a lot quicker. What'd you bring?"

I smiled and nodded over at the two tubs of mustard potato salad.

Uncle Bubba looked a little confused. "That's what you brought to an Armadillo pot-luck dinner?"

"Well, yeah." I could only wonder what protocol I'd breached now. "Isn't that all right?"

"Oh, sure it is, Nephew." He smiled and clapped me on the back again. "Course it is. Now give me a hand with all this."

I picked up the first bag and opened it. Inside was simply a six-pack of cold beer. I took it out and placed it on one of the card tables. The next sack, surprisingly enough, contained another six-pack. So did the third, and by the time I'd cleared the bags off of the card table, I had quite a little beer-pyramid stacked up.

When I looked over at Uncle Bubba, I saw that he had the same thing. I couldn't help but laugh a little—I think I was beginning to understand the meeting secrets of the Honorable Order of the Armadillo just a little bit better. As we adjourned for the evening, I saw that the parade committee was huddled over in one corner, presumably starting to hatch whatever plan my uncle had surely come up with. I just shook my head. This Fourth of July parade was probably going to be one to remember. I gathered up the last few fajita wings to take home for a late-night snack and left the fellows to their scheming.

Fajita Wings

20 chicken wings
¼ cup lime juice
1 tsp cumin
½ tsp salt
½ tsp garlic salt
½ tsp oregano
¾ tsp cayenne pepper
2 Tbsp diced cilantro

Mix all of the non-wing ingredients together and pour into a glass bowl. Make a few slices in each chicken wing, enough to let the marinade soak in well. Add the wings to the marinade and refrigerate overnight. When you get ready to cook them, remove the wings from the bowl and save the marinade. Coat a baking pan with a non-stick vegetable spray, then arrange the wings on it and let them bake at 375 degrees for about 45 minutes or until the wings are done. During the course of cooking, take the wings out and brush with marinade a few times. When they're ready, discard any remaining marinade.

A Red, White, and Blue Fourth

The Fourth arrived before I could find out what Uncle Bubba and his committee were cooking up for the parade. I went over to the town square early that day, partially to find out what the Armadillos had in store, but mostly because I'd promised Aunt Irma I'd look after her biscotti stand while she rode on the Cut Plug Garden Club float.

Several folks had set up tables to sell arts and crafts, and my aunt had taken the opportunity to sell some of the wonderful Italian biscotti cookies that she made. When I found her booth, I saw that Uncle Bubba was getting industrious as well. He had turned out three huge pans of chicken wings for sale. A sign read: *Red, White, and Blue wings*. Sure enough, each pan had one of the three different hues.

At the moment, Aunt Irma was doing the better business since the biscotti went so well with early-morning coffee, but I knew the wings would start moving swiftly around lunchtime.

"Well, hello there, Nephew!" Aunt Irma called as she saw me approaching. "I'm awful glad you're here. The ladies at the garden club are going to give my spot on the float away if I don't hurry!"

I gave her a quick hug. "Don't worry about a thing. I'll take care of the booth until you get back."

She reached up and kissed me on my cheek. As much as I loved my aunt, I didn't like it at all when she did that. I always ended up with a smear of lipstick on my face and the

overbearing scent of her perfume that seemed to hang in the air around me for the next half-hour.

"I do appreciate it, Nephew. There's a price sheet on the table, and here's my change purse." She thrust a black bag into my hands, and it had the heavy feel of coins.

Before I could say another word, she was gone, and I was quickly pulled into the role of shopkeeper. The good folks of Cut Plug were lined up to get her biscotti, and she was doing a steady business. I even sold an occasional wing or two, something that surprised me that early in the morning.

The day wore on, with quite a gathering for the big parade. By noon the focus of the booth had shifted from biscotti to wings, and Uncle Bubba was getting rave reviews. I also noticed that folks were starting to take their places on the roofs of the buildings in the town square.

The buzz of the crowd was growing, and it was at its climax when the first strains of "Stars and Stripes Forever" echoed from a few streets over. The Cut Plug High School Fighting Opossum Band had fired up a patriotic tune to start the parade.

The sound was getting closer and closer, and just as I started to pick out little Amy Seaton trying to hit the high notes on her piccolo, Buck came wandering into the booth.

"Hey, Bubba's doing pretty good with his wings!" He appeared to be genuinely excited about that fact and quickly began to survey the trays. "So the blue cornmeal wings are selling the best. Bubba thought they would."

"Yeah, well, I was surprised by the fact that he even had them here." I shrugged my shoulders. "I thought this was just going to be Aunt Irma's biscotti booth."

Buck grinned. "Naw, Bubba thought this would be a good way to introduce his wing business to the world. In fact, that kind of plays into the Armadillo float for the parade."

The pageant unfolded before us as we spoke. It was led by Cut Plug's mayor, Ernestine Harrington. She was the first female mayor in the history of the town, and her victory had been controversial among some of the town fathers. At the moment, she sat in the back seat of her husband's convertible and waved at the crowd.

Mr. Underwood had set up a microphone and speakers in front of his hardware store. That made him the unofficial emcee of the day, so it was no surprise to hear his voice booming out above the din of the crowd. "Ladies and Gentlemen, welcome to Cut Plug's Fourth of July Celebration. Leading the parade is our distinguished mayor, Mrs. Ernestine Harrington!" A smattering of applause rippled through the crowd.

Next came the twenty-three-person high school marching band. All that took my mind off Buck's comment for a moment, but it didn't take long before I realized he'd said that Uncle Bubba had somehow tied the float and his chicken wing restaurant together. "So, Buck." I hesitated. "What is the Honorable Order of the Armadillo contribution to this event?"

Buck just winked. "You're about to find out."

Mr. Underwood's voice rose above the sound of the band. "Let's give these kids a big round of applause, folks!" The crowd complied with enthusiasm.

As the last band member went by, the siren from the fire truck that was following them cut loose. The fellows from the Volunteer Fire Department were all on board Cut Plug's one and only fire engine, a 1960s model that the town bought from Tater Springs when they upgraded their equipment a few years back. The boys had all the lights flashing on it, and the people just loved it. The firefighters were given a tremendous ovation. I knew that Mr. Underwood was torn between riding with his fellow volunteers and emceeing the parade, and as the red truck passed, he snapped to attention and gave them an impressive salute.

After the truck passed by, he went back to his duties, and I heard Mr. Underwood trying to compete with the sirens. He called out, "Let's get ready for Cut Plug's high school cheering squad!" It was a bit premature, since Melissa Anderson's mom, who was carefully driving the car that they were all riding on, had the speed set a little slower than the rest of the parade. She was obviously afraid of an accident: two cheerleaders were perched on the hood of the car, two more were on the roof with their feet hanging off on the sides, and a final one waved enthusiastically while sitting on the trunk. The girls had made signs out of butcher paper that proclaimed, "Happy Fourth!" and they were taped to all sides of the car.

Right about that time, a tractor rounded the corner and turned onto the town square. Driving the tractor was Mr. Trickle. He was perched up on it like some proud peacock, and a sign was hanging on either side of the tractor that proudly proclaimed "sponsored by *Cut Plug First National Bank*."

95

The tractor was obviously pulling a float, and its nose began to creep around the corner. I figured that the base of it was someone's hay trailer. The ladies had put a large ruffle around the bottom to hide the wheels and frame, and on the side were large, sparkling letters that spelled out: *L-I-B-E-R-T-Y*. On the front of the hay trailer was Marianne Trickle, who was wearing an old-timey dress that appeared to be made of small blue flowers and was holding a sign that said *Women's Rights*! I looked over to Buck, who guessed, "Is that the Susan B. Anthony lady from the coin?" kind of hesitantly.

I nodded—it had to be. She was surrounded by a blanket of colorful flowers, which flowed back into a field of bright yellow. It only took me a second to see that the ladies had used small yellow flowers on the center of the float and around Mrs. Anester, who sat in a chair holding a flag made out of red, white, and blue petals. "Betsy Ross," Buck whispered in my ear. I turned and nodded. That one I'd gotten on my own. It only made sense that Mrs. Anester got to ride on the float, since she was the one who talked that town-lawyer husband of hers into letting the parade take place at all.

The end of the float finally came into view, and it was extravagant. A covering of blue flowers, apparently representing water, surrounded a small island of brown. In the center of this island stood my Aunt Irma. She was draped in a green robe made out of ivy, and her skin glistened with a tint of emerald makeup. In a single upstretched hand, she held a green torch that had at least a dozen sparklers burning in it. Aunt Irma was Cut Plug's answer to the Statue of Liberty, and I couldn't help but feel a little proud.

"Aawww-llll right, citizens," Underwood's amplified voice boomed, "let's all salute the Garden Club's celebration of liberty!"

The float was moving down the street in front of me when I felt Buck's elbow jab me in the side. "Look at this, now. Here comes our float."

A huge, gray blob, roughly the size of a pickup truck, slowly came into view. It was swaying slightly from side to side and looked a little unstable. There was a small head with a small snout on front, and it had two front feet reaching around like arms. In one claw it held an American flag, and in the other, it held what appeared to be a large chicken wing. Trailing behind the monstrosity was a thick, gray tail. "Oh my Lord." I said slowly.

"So what ya think?" Buck looked like a proud father. "It's a giant armadillo!"

Of course, I knew that it was an armadillo—at least a representation of one. They had even painted black stripes from one side to the other to look like the plating of an armadillo. Still, at a glance the whole contraption looked like a giant gray blob. As best as I could guess, Uncle Bubba had built some sort of giant frame to ride on his pickup—the very bottoms of the wheels were still visible. The rest of the truck was covered by the makeshift armadillo, which was probably a fabrication of chicken wire and plaster.

"Buck, it looks like you fellows at least gave it a good try." And it did. Uncle Bubba's chicken wing in that outstretched front claw was a wonderful touch.

We heard Mr. Underwood once again. "And now, folks, the Honorable Order of the Armadillos honor the Fourth with their, uh," his voice just trailed off. "Their Armadillo!" he finally added.

Buck was clapping wildly, when he suddenly stopped. His eyes were locked on something out in the street.

I followed his gaze and immediately saw what had caught his attention—Uncle Bubba's armadillo was wobbling wildly, and from inside of the aberrance, even over the noise of the crowd and the strains of music from the band in the distance, I could hear a muffled argument taking place. "Buck, who's driving that thing?" I just had to ask, because something wasn't right.

"Well," he started, never taking his eyes off of the giant armadillo, "Your uncle's behind the wheel, but because of all the two-by-fours used in the frame, we couldn't cut a peep-hole out for him."

I got that feeling in the pit of my stomach again, the one that creeps up every time I get the suspicion that Uncle Bubba's doing something a little off-kilter. "I know I'm gonna regret asking this, Buck, but how is Uncle Bubba seeing to steer that contraption?"

"Well, that's part of the whole beauty of its design. Skeeter's standing up in the bed of the truck, right behind the cab, looking through a small hole in the front." He pointed to the gray glob. "See it right there, near the top?"

Sure enough, there it was, just at the top of the armor in the top of the plaster animal. It was small enough that, without Buck's help, I never would have noticed it.

Buck continued on with his explanation. "When it's time for Bubba to go left, Skeeter pounds on the left side of the cab. He does just the opposite for a right turn."

I noticed that the first part of the parade was slowing. "So, Buck, how does Skeeter signal Uncle Bubba when its time to stop?"

A blank expression was instantly on his face, and I could tell that he was searching for an answer that he didn't have. "I dunno. I figured Bubba and Skeeter worked all that out."

I wasn't that optimistic. The band had apparently come to a halt somewhere down the line, because I could see the sousaphone players stopped down the street—the rest of the band was hidden by a turn around the town square. The fire truck halted, giving the volunteers a chance to sound the siren once again. Behind that, Trickle slowed the tractor, and the Garden

Club's float had almost come to a stop. The ladies were still smiling and waving, unaware that Uncle Bubba's armadillo-mobile was bearing down on them like a Sherman tank.

"Buck, I'm not sure that Uncle Bubba's gonna stop!" I would have run out of the booth to try and help, but I don't think I could have gotten through the shell of the critter in time to warn my uncle. Still, it was obvious that a commotion was taking place in the animal's innards.

It rocked with even a greater ferocity and barreled toward the Cut Plug Garden Club's Liberty float with a vengeance. When it was thirty yards away, I saw a singular fist poke through the top of the armadillo's shell, and it continued to gyrate around, breaking the surrounding plaster.

Skeeter's head finally popped through the top, and he quickly surveyed the situation. A sudden expression of alarm crossed his face, and he yelled, "Bubba!" at the top of his lungs.

It was a futile effort. The giant armadillo plowed into the Liberty float like Grant took Richmond. For a brief moment, I was terrified for Aunt Irma's safety, but when I saw that the ladies had been propelled up into the air, I knew they would land safely in the bed of flowers spread over the surface of the trailer.

What I didn't anticipate was exactly what would happen next.

When Aunt Irma landed, so did the torch—right in the middle of Betsy Ross' flower flag. I have no idea what kind of cloth those ladies used underneath the flowers, but the sparklers ignited it immediately. Mrs. Anester, who had come to rest there in the middle of the float, let out a blood-curdling wail. Her natural instincts must have taken over. She flung the flaming blanket away from her with all her might. Unfortunately, it landed at the feet of Marianne Trickle. She was resting on the side of the field of flowers at the front part of the float, which had apparently broken her fall.

The flames caught up around her and quickly spread to her costume. She leapt to her feet and started screaming like a banshee, but at least she had the presence of mind to whip off the flower-petal dress.

The Cut Plug Garden Club's glorious salute to liberty was in shambles. Someone was helping Aunt Irma down from the trailer, Mrs. Anester was climbing off on her own, and Marianne Trickle was just standing in the middle of the whole thing in a scarlet red bra, garter belt, stockings, and French-cut panties.

As the volunteer firemen beat out the flames, Cut Plug's best-kept secret was suddenly revealed. On Mrs. Trickle's right cheek, just peeking out from the red fabric, was a tattoo of a teddy bear. I think she was too frightened to be embarrassed, but in the city of Cut Plug, one thing is for certain: People will never look at her the same way. There was apparently a wild side to Marianne Trickle.

When the good banker turned around and saw what was happening, he floored the tractor and sped off down a side street. Skeeter was making a quick evaluation of the situation, and his head suddenly popped back down through the hole. I can only assume that he was giving Uncle Bubba the correct pounding-code on the cab of the truck, because the armadillo-mobile backed up, then took a right down the alley by Mr. Underwood's Hardware store.

As it disappeared, I figured it would be some time before Cut Plug saw the giant armadillo again. It might even be longer before Aunt Irma was speaking to Uncle Bubba, but I knew for a fact that I probably wouldn't be seeing Marianne Trickle out in public for a while.

There in the booth, though, I did a pretty good business with Uncle Bubba's patriotic wings. Everyone was laughing, talking, and buying chicken wings. If you'd like to make the red, white, and blue wings we sold that day, there's no need to wait for the Fourth—any occasion will do.

Red Hot Wings

20 chicken wings
1 stick butter
½ tsp black pepper
½ tsp red pepper
½ tsp white pepper
½ tsp garlic powder
¼ cup of your favorite pepper sauce
2 cups flour

Melt the butter in a pan over low heat, then stir in the spices and the pepper sauce. Rinse the chicken wings in water, and pat them on a paper towel to remove any excess water. Roll each wing in flour, then use a deep fryer or skillet with about an inch of olive oil to fry the wings.

When they're ready, dip each wing in the sauce, coating them completely. Let the finished wings sit at room temperature for about 10 minutes before serving.

White Almond Chicken Wings

20 chicken wings
¾ cup flour
2 eggs
1 cup ground almonds
1 cup bread crumbs
1 tsp cornstarch
½ tsp basil
½ tsp white pepper
1 tsp salt

Mix all the dry ingredients together in one bowl, then beat the eggs together in another. Coat each wing with egg, then roll them in the dry mixture until they are completely coated.

Preheat your oven to 375 degrees, and bake the wings on a greased cookie sheet for about 45 minutes. Since all ovens vary, start watching them after half an hour to make sure they don't burn.

Blue Cornmeal Wings

20 chicken wings
½ cup lime juice
½ cup olive oil
2 Tbsp crushed red pepper flakes
½ cup blue cornmeal
2 Tbsp flour
½ tsp salt
½ tsp cumin
⅛ tsp black pepper

Combine the lime juice, oil, and red pepper flakes in a large bowl. Add the wings, and make sure they're completely coated. Cover the bowl and refrigerate for at least 3 hours, but overnight would be preferred. As they're marinating, when you think of it, swirl the mixture around in the bowl.

Before cooking the wings, mix the remaining ingredients in another bowl, and coat the marinated wings in the cornmeal mixture. Arrange them on a greased cookie sheet.

Preheat oven to 375 degrees, and bake the wings for approximately 45 minutes.

Head Over Heels

*T*hankfully, summers are long in Cut Plug, so the whole Fourth of July incident fell by the wayside. After all, no one was hurt. The only possible exception might be Marianne Trickle's modesty. Uncle Bubba came through it all unscathed, even with all the trouble he'd caused.

That night, after the parade, I met Uncle Bubba down at Junior Newton's barn with Buck and Skeeter. With a little help from Junior we got the giant armadillo's frame off my uncle's truck in short order. We decided that the barn would be a good place for the huge armadillo to live.

I got invited over to Uncle Bubba's house a week or so later, since he wanted to fix dinner for me in appreciation of helping with the armadillo, and for manning their booth during the parade.

My aunt and uncle both made a killing that day, and while I wasn't sure what Aunt Irma was going to do with her money, Uncle Bubba had officially started the Chicken Wing Restaurant fund.

On this particular evening I was being treated to a wonderful batch of honey Worcestershire wings, and while my uncle was fixing them, Aunt Irma and I were sitting at the kitchen table visiting. She was going on and on about how beautiful the Cut Plug Garden Club's float was.

I reminded her what an untimely end it had, but she just laughed harder.

"I tell you, boy, Marianne still hasn't come out of her house," she cackled. "Imagine her, wearing all those fancy underthings just like a big-city floozy! And a tattoo on her bottom—I can't wait to hear the tale behind that one!"

I couldn't help but chuckle myself. Just as I was about to ask if anyone had even talked to her, there was a knock on the front door. Before anyone could react we heard it open, and Skeeter's voice rang through the house. "Bubba! Irma! Ya'll home?"

My uncle yelled out, "Back here in the kitchen!"

In a moment Skeeter joined us. Aunt Irma pulled out one of the chairs at the table with us, and he sat down.

He removed the ever-present gimmie cap and laid it down on the table. "Sorry to barge in on you folks, especially during supper and all."

Aunt Irma reached out and patted him on the shoulder. "Oh, don't you worry about that. You know how my Bubba cooks—always plenty of food."

"That's right!" Bubba chimed in. "We're having some honey Worcestershire wings, so if that fits your mouth this evening, then stay and eat with us."

Skeeter just sat there a second. "Well, I really needed a word with you, Bubba. I've got a problem."

My uncle stopped working on the wings. "A problem? What's wrong?"

Skeeter was silent again and then glanced from me to Aunt Irma a few times before standing up and whispering something in Uncle Bubba's ear.

Uncle Bubba suddenly doubled over, laughing. "A woman? You need my help with a woman?" He laughed even louder, then clapped his friend on the back so hard I thought Skeeter would sail across the room. "Why, Skeeter's got a girlfriend!"

Aunt Irma just beamed. "Well do declare, Skeeter, it's about time. You were collecting ex-sweethearts there for so long, I thought you'd given up on finding a wife. Now don't keep us in suspense—who's the lucky gal?"

Skeeter was beet-red, and you could just feel the embarrassment beaming off of him. He was looking at the floor and mumbled something that I couldn't make out.

Bubba clapped him on the back again. "C'mon now, Skeeter, out with it. Who is she?"

In a low voice, he said, "Effie Marie Callahan."

"Callahan?" Aunt Irma's brow wrinkled, and a disapproving scowl crossed her face. "She's the new lady truck driver over at the cement plant, isn't she." It was an accusation, not a question. As her eyes narrowed, my aunt firmly decreed, "Skeeter, you leave her alone—I hear that woman is rougher than a peanut pattie on the goober side."

I'd met Effie when she started at the plant last year, and she seemed nice enough. She was falling prey to the curse of any small town: No one trusted a person new to the town, and unless you were born here, by definition, you were new to town.

Uncle Bubba just shook his head. "Pay no attention to her, Skeeter. You look like you're head over heels in love with that girl, so we've got to get you fixed up. Why don't you come with me." Bubba grabbed his arm and started toward the living room. He looked back over his shoulder at me. "You've seen me fix these particular wings a hundred times, Nephew. Why don't you take over?"

Without another word, he and Skeeter were gone. I realized what an honor had just been bestowed on me. My uncle never allowed anyone to infringe on his cooking. He'd just turned the reins over to me, though, so I took my place at the oven and gave it my best effort.

Aunt Irma sat there carrying on and on about Effie Marie Callahan, and just as I took the wings out of the oven for the last time, Uncle Bubba and Skeeter walked triumphantly back in.

My uncle walked over and inspected the wings. He picked one up and sniffed of it, then took a bite, and finally smiled approvingly. He continued to munch on the wing, and with a full mouth said, "Well, we got Romeo all fixed up!"

Skeeter shrugged sheepishly. "I hope so, anyway. Bubba helped me write a poem for her." He extended his hand toward me, holding a piece of notebook paper. "Read it and see what you think."

I took the poem, and in my best oratory voice, begin to vocalize its melodic strains:

"Effie, oh Effie, you make my heart beat,
from my best gimmie cap to the boots on my feet.

When I saw you driving that big rig of yours
I just had to meet you, and that is for sure.

The angelic vision of you 'hind the wheel
makes me know for certain, it's love that I feel.

You're so much more beautiful than all of my ex-'s,
you're the prettiest girl in Cut Plug, Texas."

My eyes met Aunt Irma's, and we both wondered what to say. I looked over at Skeeter. His eyes were moist, and I'd swear that his lip was trembling a little. "Skeeter, it's perfect. Best of luck to you."

Skeeter quickly made his apologies for supper and shot out of the house. I was pretty sure he was going out on the town, searching for his true love.

Meanwhile, the three of us ate the wings: honey Worcestershire and Dijon orange. In fact, I'd swear they tasted even better since I had a hand in making them.

Honey Worcestershire Wings

20 chicken wings
½ cup honey
¼ cup Worcestershire sauce
1 tsp garlic powder

The honey Worcestershire wings are wonderful in their simplicity. These can usually be made with ingredients that are already in anyone's pantry. The process is just as easy and is the same for the Dijon orange wings.

Dijon Orange Wings

20 chicken wings
4 Tbsp Dijon mustard
3 Tbsp frozen orange juice concentrate
½ cup soy sauce

Mix all the ingredients, except for the wings, in a bowl. Add the wings and marinate in the refrigerator overnight. Preheat the oven to 375 degrees, and spread out the wings on a cookie sheet that has been coated with a vegetable spray. If you happen to be making both recipes at the same time, use two sheets so the flavors won't combine. Bake the wings for 45 minutes to an hour, basting with the marinade every 15 minutes.

The Great Hospital Guerilla Invasion

After almost a week, I was still waiting to hear about Skeeter's conquests or failures in the arena of love. I'd been observing them both at the cement plant, and for the life of me I couldn't tell whether he'd made any moves or not.

It had been a particularly tiring day, and I was looking forward to getting home and just standing in the shower for a very long time. I got to the parking lot, though, and there was a piece of paper tucked under one of the windshield wipers on my truck. It said: *Nephew, meet me at the hospital, nine tonight!—Bubba.*

Cut Plug didn't have a doctor's office, much less a hospital, so for any of those needs a person had to travel a good thirty miles to the nearest big city. I assumed that was what Uncle Bubba meant, so I figured I'd drive over and try to find him.

I fixed a bite of supper, cleaned up, and headed out of town. It was almost nine o'clock. The hospital was right off the interstate, and it didn't take much to spot my uncle's pickup truck in the parking lot. I drove into an adjacent parking space, so that our driver's side windows were next to each other. We rolled them down simultaneously. "So what's going on, Uncle Bubba?"

"Well, Nephew, the doc put Mr. Patterson in the hospital yesterday. He's in the Guarded Care area, and since I'm not family, they won't let me in to see him."

I immediately registered the concern in his voice. My uncle was trying to play it casual, but deep inside I knew that he was worried about his compadre. "So, what's the plan?" I asked.

He grinned, obviously happy that I was already on board without even hearing what he was scheming. Uncle Bubba smiled. "Glad you're with me, Nephew. Now quick, put these on." He handed me a set of green scrubs like the surgeons on TV wear.

In my mind, my readiness to support him was more along the lines of speaking with some of the hospital administrators to get Uncle Bubba clearance to visit. I hadn't anticipated some kind of covert guerilla operation. Still, I knew this was important to him. They had never been best of friends, but a bond had grown from all of their exploits together. I figured the worst that could happen is we'd get thrown out of the hospital.

My scrubs appeared to be just the right size, so there must have been some planning on his part. "Where in the world did you get these, Uncle Bubba?"

He was pulling the scrub shirt down over his belly, and his answer was muffled for a second. "Borrowed 'em!" he finally said clearly. "When I was here last night and they wouldn't let me in, I saw a big closet of these as I was leaving, so I grabbed a set for each of us."

I was changing from my jeans to the scrubs there in the cab of my truck, but I just stopped and stared at him.

He grinned and held up his palm. "Now don't worry about anything; we're gonna return 'em just as soon as we've seen Patterson tonight."

I just shook my head. In for a penny, in for a pound, I supposed. I stepped out of my pickup to slip on the scrub shirt. Uncle Bubba joined me in a few moments.

"Here." He handed me a clip-on ID tag, which read: *Hi! My name is Irma!*

It was obviously a nametag from one of my aunt's Garden Club functions. Even in a small town like Cut Plug, the group seemed to enjoy the formality of big organizations. "Uncle Bubba, what in the heck is this?"

"I got a couple out of Irma's Garden Club drawer!" He winked. "It won't pass close inspection, but if someone sees us from a distance it'll at least look like we have some kind of ID on."

I couldn't help but sigh. This was getting more involved by the minute. "Okay, okay, let's just hurry."

Before he closed the door to his truck, he brought out a small bag and a large hand saw. "Nephew, I guess I'm as ready as I'm ever gonna be."

We started walking across the parking lot toward the hospital, and my curiosity was getting the best of me. "I've just got to ask, Uncle Bubba. Just what the heck are you carrying that old saw for?"

He burst out laughing. "Nephew, nothing'll perk old Patterson up faster than a good laugh. Once I saw we were going to be dressing up like doctors, I figured we'd make the best of the situation." He shook the saw, and as the gleaming blade flexed back and forth, it made a horrible, metallic howling sound. "I'm gonna scare the stuffin' out of that old man."

"Okay," I said hesitantly. The wisdom of the plan escaped me, since the whole idea was to not attract attention, but I let it go. "So what's in the bag, Uncle Bubba?"

"A sure cure!" he said with a grin. "Irma was telling me that she'd read an article about the healing powers of garlic. It's supposed to do everything from boosting your immune system to clearing out your arteries. I'm not quite sure what's wrong with Patterson, but I figure that this ought to fix him up."

Once we got in through a side entrance, my uncle grabbed a gurney that was parked in the hallway. "Help me with this, Nephew. This'll lend a little credibility to our get-ups."

III

He pulled back the sheet, carefully laid the saw down, then covered it back up smoothly. It took him a little longer to figure out where to put the wings so they wouldn't be noticeable. Being as resourceful as my uncle was, he quickly tore a hole through the top of the sack and hung it on a hook on the underside of the gurney. Lord only knows what was really supposed to hang there.

Uncle Bubba then grabbed the front and headed down the hall, and I reluctantly started pushing it from the rear. We were on the move. I felt a little like a fellow standing in a hole who had just been handed a shovel and was starting to dig deeper.

We were cruising through at a pretty fair clip, and no one had even noticed us, much less challenged our presence. All of a sudden I got a little concerned. "Uncle Bubba, you do know where we're going, don't you?" I could only imagine us having to do a room-to-room search of the hospital.

"Not a problem!" he said confidently. "I believe it'll be on the second floor, so all we have to do is get to an elevator. The nurse at the front desk last night told me that the Guarded Care unit was the first fifteen rooms up there.

I had visited a few people here in the hospital over the years, but for the life of me I had no idea where we were going. Hopefully, Uncle Bubba did. It was late enough that the corridors were pretty much deserted. We dashed down them in our medical scrubs, sporting clip-on badges identifying both of us as a lady named Irma.

We found an elevator and managed to ride up without running into anyone. As we rolled the gurney out into the second floor corridor, Uncle Bubba pointed to a sign that said *201—215* and had an arrow pointing to the left. He pulled us in that direction, but as we proceeded down the hallway, something just didn't seem right.

I looked around. "Uh, Uncle Bubba."

"Shhhh!" he hissed. "Not so loud, Nephew. Do you want us to get caught?"

"Of course not." I don't think that I've ever uttered truer words. "But if this is Guarded Care, shouldn't they have a nurse's station out here? This is just a regular hospital corridor."

My uncle dismissed my concerns with a wave of his hand. "Naw, not with all the newfangled computerized equipment they've got these days." As we approached the end of the hallway, he began to slow. "I think this is it—the nurse said that he was in room 203." We stopped in front of the door. He dug around in the pocket of his scrubs, and finally produced a cloth mask.

I was surprised at how fast he tied it on. In just a matter of a minute, he was masked like a surgeon. With one hand he eased the door open, and with the other he pulled the saw out from under the sheet.

My uncle gave me a big wink, then jumped into the room. He began shaking that saw fiercely, and it's rhythmic pulses were deafening. So much for being discreet. Uncle Bubba then hollered, "Get ready, 'cause we're here to operate!"

I stepped inside to see Mr. Patterson's reaction. To my horror, a little old woman was in the hospital bed, the covers pulled up tightly under her chin, her eyes wide in fright. She looked like she was two hundred years old if she was a day.

There was a brief moment of silence when my uncle saw that something was wrong. He stood there frozen, the saw over his head, his eyes opening ever wider as realization came over him.

I never would have guessed that old woman could scream so loud. Her voice wound up like the siren on a state trooper's patrol car, and in a singular movement, she threw back the covers and charged us. Uncle Bubba and I both yelled and instinctively jumped out of the way.

That woman ran between us and kept going out into the hallway. I heard her scream fading, but I couldn't even guess where
she finally ended up.

I looked over at my uncle, and he just said, "Uh-oh." We
must have had the same idea at the same time, because we both
turned and ran. The saw clattered to the floor behind me, so I
assumed Bubba had ditched it to make better time.

The stairs were only a little further than the elevator, and we
opted for those. When the door shut behind us in the stairwell,
we heaved a collective sigh of relief.

Uncle Bubba had a pensive expression, like he was reaching back into his mind. "You know, maybe that nurse told me it was room 302, instead. C'mon!" He turned and started up the stairs.

"Uncle Bubba, do you really think that's a good idea?" At this point, my vote would have been to get out as quickly as possible. "I mean, you don't even have the garlic wings anymore!"

He just kept going up. "I'll make up another batch. Right now, I'm not leaving until I get to check on Patterson."

All I could do was shrug my shoulders and follow him up the stairs. It was a genuine shame about the wings; medicinal or not, I knew they would have been delicious.

For a second, I thought about going back down to get the ones Uncle Bubba had left with the gurney. It was probably better not to tempt fate, though, so I decided just to let them be.

Sure enough, Patterson's room was number 302, and there was a nurse's station not far from it that served the Guarded Care rooms. Room 302 was fortunately just around the corner from it, which afforded us a bit of privacy.

I nodded at the door. "Why don't you go in and spend a few minutes with Mr. Patterson, and I'll stand guard. If you hear me knock on the door, then it's time for us to get out of here."

Uncle Bubba nodded once, pushed open the door, and disappeared inside. I crossed my arms to hide the Irma badge, and just tried to look nonchalant.

A good ten minutes passed, and I'd occasionally hear peals of laughter through the door. I was standing there quietly, wondering how long Uncle Bubba was going to chance staying, when a doctor in a white coat rounded the corner.

He stopped and looked at me suspiciously, finally saying, "I thought I knew most everyone here at the hospital. Are you new?"

I stammered a second. "Uh, brand new in fact." I was nodding my head, and I extended my hand in greeting. "Pleased to meet you."

The doctor just stood there. "Or could you be one of the two orderlies who've been getting into mischief this evening? Was that you, Mr.," he reached out and pulled up my ID. "Mr. Irma?"

Aunt Irma had always said that honesty was the best policy, so I decided to just tell him the truth. I took a deep breath. "Look, doc, the man in there is a person that my uncle thinks a lot of. The nurse out front wouldn't let Uncle Bubba in to see him, so I agreed to help him get up here with a few covert tactics." I couldn't help but give him a sheepish smile. "I guess in the course of things, we inadvertently caused a little ruckus."

The doctor nodded his head, seemingly satisfied with my explanation and honesty. "Tell you what—why don't you give your uncle another five minutes or so. Mr. Patterson could use the company."

I stuck out my hand again, and this time he shook it. "Thanks, doc. It'll mean the world to my uncle."

"Well, it won't hurt Mr. Patterson either." A solemn look crossed his face. "I guess you've heard about his condition."

Something told me I didn't want to hear this. Still, I figured I should get any info I could for Uncle Bubba. "No, I can't say that I have."

He glanced around the hallway, then moved in closer towards me. "Look, I probably shouldn't say anything at all, since you're not family. Best we can tell, though, Mr. Patterson really doesn't have any relations. Your uncle's going to have to do." He dropped the tone of his voice considerably. "You see, Mr. Patterson's condition is very serious. There's just no good way to say this—he doesn't have a whole lot longer left in him."

The statement took me aback, and for a minute I could only stand there staring at the doctor. "Can't you treat him with some kind of medicine? Isn't there anything you can do?"

He looked away and then shook his head. "No, I'm afraid not. It's just a matter of time. I wish there was something I could do." There was a sad glisten in his eyes. "I feel so helpless at times like this. Even as far as medicine has come, there are some lines that we just can't get across yet." He reached out and thumped my Irma badge. "Tell you what, I'm going to leave special instructions at the front desk to allow your uncle to visit as much as he wants. That way the two of you can dress a little more casual next time." He smiled, then turned and walked away.

My gut hurt. I was going to have to break the news to Uncle Bubba, and I hated to have to do that. As I stood there in the hallway, I don't know if I've ever felt that much alone.

In a few minutes the door opened, and Uncle Bubba popped through. He called a final farewell to Mr. Patterson, then said, "Let's get out of here, Nephew, before we get caught."

I fell in behind him as we took the stairs down. I couldn't think of the right words to say, and oddly enough, Uncle Bubba was uncharacteristically quiet. That fact alone bothered me— my uncle was never at a loss for words.

When we got out to our trucks, we changed back into our regular clothes, and Uncle Bubba offered to take the scrubs back up and leave them in a hallway.

I looked at him for a second and finally got my courage up. "Uncle Bubba, there's something I have to tell you." He stood there staring at me. Somehow, I sensed that he already knew. "See, while you were in there with Mr. Patterson, I ran into his doctor. He...he said," my voice broke, and I had to stop for a second.

My uncle took a deep, slow breath. "That old boy's not going to make it, is he?"

I shook my head slowly. "No, Uncle, he's not. The doctor said there wasn't anything else he could do. He's leaving your name at the front desk, though, so at least you'll be able to get in to see Mr. Patterson without us having to dress up and all."

We stood out there without another word, and Uncle Bubba finally smiled. I could see the pain on his face. A single tear rolled down his cheek, and he swallowed hard. "Nephew, why don't you head back home. I'm gonna drop these scrubs back inside the door before I go."

I reached over and hugged Uncle Bubba as hard as I could, and I could hear him sniffing the tears away. When I let go, I climbed into the truck, started the engine, and drove away. My uncle needed to be alone.

Just to make sure he was okay, I made a long, slow circle around the outside of the hospital parking lot. When I made the loop, I saw that he'd returned to his truck but was just sitting down on the curb beside it.

I turned out of the parking lot and decided I'd drop in on Aunt Irma on the way home, just to let her know. It was probably going to be a long night for my uncle.

Garlic Wings

20 chicken wings
4 Tbsp finely chopped garlic
1 cup olive oil
2 dashes Tabasco pepper sauce
1 cup grated Parmesan cheese
1 cup Italian style bread crumbs
⅛ tsp salt
¼ tsp pepper
¼ tsp rosemary
¼ tsp thyme
¼ tsp oregano

Even with all the ingredients, this is a simple recipe. Start by preheating your oven to 375 degrees. After you've chopped the garlic, put it and the oil and pepper sauce in a blender, combine on the high setting, then transfer the mixture to a small bowl. Next combine the cheese, bread crumbs, and spices in another small bowl.

Coat each wing in the garlic mixture, then roll in the bread crumbs. Arrange the wings on a cookie sheet and bake for 45 minutes to an hour or until done.

While I can't speak for the healing power of this recipe, there are volumes that have been dedicated to medicinal qualities of garlic. Perhaps this is a cure-all that will revolutionize medicine as we know it, or maybe it's just a delicious recipe. I don't know, and I don't care; they have been a staple of my diet since that night.

Backyard Leaf Burning Revelations

I loved the smell of fall. The weather was growing cooler, and the good folks of Cut Plug were starting to burn wood in their fireplaces.

As the leaves collected under the trees, homeowners would rake them into piles and spend a Saturday afternoon burning them, holding a rake in one hand and a hose in the other. It was also the busy season for the Cut Plug Volunteer Fire Department, which got called out to someone's house at least once a month to help put out the drying grass that had accidentally caught fire.

On Friday, my uncle found me in the cafeteria at the plant and said that he was going to burn some leaves the next afternoon. He told me that if I'd stop by he would cook up a batch of Tandoori wings for us. Now I have no idea where Uncle Bubba learned to cook a dish that's native to India, but he does them up right. Needless to say, I was going over at the appointed time.

It amazed me that there was just something in males that drew us to the act of standing around a fire, watching it burn. There must be some kind of primeval carryover buried in our DNA. I've got to admit, though, it was great. Every party I'd ever been to was like that: The fellows would stand out in the backyard around the grill, just watching the fire, while the women sat inside and shared their innermost feelings.

I showed up at Uncle Bubba's on Saturday just as he was raking the last of the leaves from his yard into a large, although manageable, pile. Skeeter was standing there as well, and from where I was standing in the driveway, both of them looked pretty low.

Aunt Irma was coming out of the back door, carrying a plate full of chicken wings. I detected the slight, exotic scent of the Tandoori wings, and I couldn't help but stop, raise my eyebrows, and give her a hopeful look.

She just laughed and held the plate out. "Well, course you can have one, Nephew. Dig in!"

I picked a drumette off the top and enjoyed the exquisite taste as I bit into it.

"Now, come on." She took off across the backyard. "Help me talk some sense into these two."

"What's wrong, Aunt Irma?" I asked with my mouth still full, an indiscretion that I hoped she would overlook.

"Oh, Skeeter's pining away over that no-account truck drivin' girl from the plant, and your uncle has finally lost his mind completely."

I followed her to the area where Uncle Bubba had set up a card table and four lawn chairs a few yards away from the pile of leaves.

"Hey, Nephew." I could tell that he was a little down from the slow, half-hearted effort he was using to get the last of the leaves together. "Glad you could stop by."

Aunt Irma put the wings on the card table. "It's a good thing you did! You wouldn't believe what dang fool thing your uncle was thinking about doing." She shot my uncle a frustrated look as he approached and took a wing. "Just you tell him, Bubba. Tell your nephew what your big plan was!"

He kind of smiled half-heartedly. "Aw, it was just an idea. Skeeter here's the one with the big problem."

Although Skeeter had joined us and was helping himself to a chicken wing, he just wasn't himself. His shoulders were drooping, there was a frown on his face, and he was just picking at the drumette.

"Okay, Skeeter," I prompted. "Fill me in. What's going on that's got you so down?"

"Well, I guess it's Effie Marie." He shrugged and bowed his head. "Things just kind of went haywire."

I waited for more of an explanation, but when none came, I decided that I'd have to prompt him. "So did you read her your poem?"

Uncle Bubba snickered. "Go ahead, Skeeter. Tell him about it!"

Aunt Irma shot him a stern look, and my uncle quickly turned his attention back to the wing he was eating.

Skeeter shook his head. "You know, I thought I really had something there with that poem. Since I was too scared to recite it to her face, though, I waited until she was out on a cement haul in her truck. I know Alfred the dispatcher pretty well, so I went in the office yesterday morning and asked him if he would put the radio on Effie's frequency for me." He sat down in one of the lawn chairs, as if telling the tale was draining strength from him. "He said that the radio was already on her frequency, so I just made up some excuse to leave and hid right outside the office. See, I knew that about the same time every morning Alfred takes the newspaper to the gent's room for a while."

"Everyone knows that, Skeeter," Uncle Bubba pointed out. "You can set your clock by that fellow."

Skeeter took a cautious bite of Tandoori wing, swallowed it, then continued. "Yeah, well, I snuck into the dispatch office while he was out. It took all my courage, but I keyed the mike and recited my poem to Effie Marie. When I was done, I didn't dare wait for a reply, I just ran out."

Uncle Bubba began to chuckle. "Tell him the rest, Skeeter."

Skeeter frowned at my uncle, then continued his story. "Well, what Alfred had neglected to tell me was that the radio wasn't tuned to just Effie's signal. The plant apparently uses CB radio to communicate with the cement trucks, so everyone who was driving that day heard my poem. You wouldn't believe the ration of grief I got later in the day as the word spread. If I heard *Effie, Oh Effie* once, I musta heard it a hundred times." This was really hurting him. Skeeter was just sitting in the chair, holding his head down, not saying a word.

Finally, he spoke. "You know, Bubba, it just isn't fair. You've got Irma, and ya'll are two of the happiest people on Earth." He took a long, deep breath. "But when I find someone that I think I could really care about, I go and screw the whole thing up."

I don't know why I happened to glance over at my aunt at that moment, but I did. She was sitting there taking all this in, and there was a contemplative look in her eyes. She was seeing beyond this backyard and the simple pile of leaves. Something in Aunt Irma was changing.

Suddenly, she stood up. "Good Lord almighty, Skeeter, what do you expect, looking to Bubba for love advice. He hasn't had to court a girl since he wooed me back in high school. What you need is a woman's touch." Aunt Irma took him by the arm and pulled him to his feet. "Now you come on in the house and let's figure out how to get this girl to notice you!" She led him off like she was taking a horse to the water pond.

Uncle Bubba watched them walk away, shook his head from side to side, and let out a low whistle. "I've seen that look in her eyes before. I don't know what changed her opinion about that Effie lady, but unless I miss my guess, she's shifted into high-gear matchmaking mode. The world may not be safe for anyone for a while if she's really got her sights set on getting those two together."

I couldn't help but laugh. "You just let them alone. I want to know what Aunt Irma said was going on with you."

"Oh, that." My uncle tightened his lips and raised his eyebrows. He took a very deep breath through his nose, and let it out slowly. "I guess I had a stupid idea, and I was fool enough to mention it to Irma today."

"Shoot, Uncle Bubba, I'm sure it couldn't be any worse than some of the others you've had." Small comfort, I know, but when it came to his ideas, it was all I could muster.

"Well," he started, "the better part of the year's gone by, and I'm still not a dang bit closer to opening my wing restaurant. In fact, I've only got $437 saved up." Uncle Bubba finished the wing he was eating and tossed the bone onto the plate. "I thought I'd use it to make an investment."

"An investment?" I took another bite of Tandoori wing, knowing full well that my uncle wasn't the investment banker type.

Uncle Bubba cleared his throat. "I was gonna buy lottery tickets."

I almost spit a mouthful of chicken wing across the backyard. "You were going to do what?"

He scowled. "Well I didn't say it was a good idea, Nephew. I'm just not sure how I'm going to pull this thing together if I don't find some way to get the financing."

I couldn't help but laugh. "No wonder Aunt Irma was perturbed when I first got here." I reached over and slapped him on his knee. "Don't do anything crazy now, Uncle. We'll get you there someway."

He just smiled weakly. "I know, Nephew, I know. I just can't figure how."

"Meanwhile," I nodded back toward the house, "I wonder what Aunt Irma's got Skeeter going through in there?"

This brought a genuine laugh from Uncle Bubba. "I have absolutely no idea. Not sure that I'd want to. It's probably best, though, if we just sit out here and enjoy these wings." With that, he produced a box of matches from his pocket, struck one, and tossed it into the pile of leaves. They caught up immediately, and we both walked over to watch it burn.

In Cut Plug it's still legal to have fires in the city limits, but in your town it's probably not. Still, it won't stop you from enjoying some of the same wings we had that day!

Backyard Tandoori Chicken Wings

20 chicken wings
1 cup plain yogurt or sour cream
1 Tbsp ginger powder
1 Tbsp minced garlic
2 tsp curry powder
¼ tsp turmeric
½ tsp cumin
½ tsp dry mustard
½ tsp paprika
2 tsp red pepper flakes
3 Tbsp lemon juice
2 Tbsp olive oil

Mix all of the ingredients, except the wings, together in a bowl. Before adding the wings, make several cuts in them with a knife. Marinate the wings in the refrigerator overnight. The next day, preheat the oven to 375 degrees, and put the wings on a greased cookie sheet. Bake them for about 45 minutes or until done. Every 15 minutes baste the wings in the marinade.

The first time I had Tandoori chicken in a restaurant, I noticed it was a bright red color. I asked Uncle Bubba about this, and he said the traditional dish includes a few drops of red food coloring. That just didn't seem right to him, though, so he never adds it.

Hurricane Irma

Something odd was going on at the plant, I just didn't know what. I'd seen half a dozen men giving the sign of the Armadillo that day. None of it was aimed at me, mind you. In fact, those who had seen me watching had quickly tried to disguise what they were doing. Some jerked their hand down quickly, while others just looked up at the ceiling innocently and started scratching their ears.

I didn't really mind not being in on whatever it was. The main reason I'd put up with the Armadillo nonsense at all was just to make Uncle Bubba happy. I just shook my head and went on about my day.

By the time I left work, I was especially glad not to have any commitments—Armadillo or otherwise. The rain was starting to come down in sheets, mostly due to a hurricane that hit the coast of Texas earlier in the day. Those coastal towns down on the Gulf always took the brunt of the storm, but for the hours following the landfall, the storms swept across Texas to dump whatever force they had left.

Which was, of course, what was happening on that particular evening. I listened to the rain beating against the side of the house. It always relaxed me and gave me a warm feeling that I was safe within the confines of my shelter. There was no way I would have gotten out into the weather that night, were it not for the telephone call I received from my aunt.

"Nephew," she started, "there's trouble brewing in Cut Plug!"

Now, it seemed as though lately there was always trouble brewing in Cut Plug, but she had a fierce edge to her voice. "What's going on, Aunt Irma?"

"Well some folks are just turning the town into a regular sin city, that's what's going on!" She was hot. No doubt about it. "The Book of Ruth Bible class was meeting over at Oralee Franklin's when we got the news. Mable Matheson came in and told us her husband had heard that someone is running a gambling house! Right here in Cut Plug!"

Alarms went off in my head like the sirens on the Volunteer Fire Department's big, red ladder truck. "Uh, Aunt Irma, do you have any idea where Uncle Bubba is?" I was trying to be as nonchalant as possible with my query.

"Thank the Lord, Bubba's not involved in this. He's over at the lodge's business meeting." I could hear the relief in her voice for a second, but it turned crisp again. "Anyway, the ladies and I are going out to try to find this den of iniquity and shut it down! I just wanted to let you know where I was in case you ran across Bubba before I do. I'm going to leave him a note, but you know how he is. That man is just as likely to swing by your place as he is to come straight home from the meeting."

I took a long, deep breath. I could feel a long night coming on. "If I see him, Aunt Irma, I'll let him know." I said my good-byes and hung up the phone. My mind was already putting the pieces of the puzzle together: something up with the Armadillos, my uncle away at some business meeting, and the opportunity for money to change hands. It all added up to one of Uncle Bubba's wild schemes. I figured I had to try to rescue him, so as much as I hated to get out in this weather, I grabbed a jacket and headed for my pickup.

There wasn't even a question in my mind of where to go. I pointed the truck toward Junior Newton's barn, the unofficial Armadillo headquarters.

Sure enough, there were enough vehicles crowded around that it looked like a reasonable-sized used car lot. I snaked my way through the water and mud until I was around at the far side of the barn. Once I shut the engine off, I could hear the music and commotion coming from inside the barn, even over the steady pounding of the rain.

At that point, I figured we were safe. All I had to do was round up Uncle Bubba and get him back home before Aunt Irma found her way here. In fact, I had almost made it to the barn door, when I saw three sets of headlights coming down the country road at a full throttle.

Either it was more patrons for whatever casino had been erected in Junior Newton's barn, or that was Aunt Irma and the other good ladies from the Book of Ruth Bible class. There just wasn't a doubt in my mind. It had to be the latter.

I threw open the barn door and dashed in from the rain, but I wasn't prepared for what I saw. The barn looked as busy as any gaming room in Las Vegas. There were a handful of dice tables that were surrounded by screaming Armadillos, their fists clutching greenbacks and waving in the air.

I saw at least three roulette wheels in operation, and they seemed to be just as popular as the craps games. There were even a few tables where I wasn't quite familiar with the particular games of chance being played.

Of course, I didn't have to look very hard for Uncle Bubba. He stepped right up to greet me, dressed in his best Sunday suit. "Nephew! I had no idea that you cared for an occasional game of chance! Welcome to little Las Vegas—Cut Plug style!"

I grabbed his arm and started pulling him toward the far side of the barn. "Uncle, let's get out of here right now! There has to be a rear exit in this place." Like any barn, all the walls looked alike, and I couldn't determine a back way out.

My uncle jerked his arm away. "Now just see here, Nephew! Things are moving along just fine. As long as Irma doesn't find out what's going on here, everything will be okay!"

I spun around and looked him square in the eye. "That's the problem, Uncle! Aunt Irma and her entire Bible class are about two minutes away. We can't save everyone else, but I can at least get you out of here."

Uncle Bubba's eyes widened, and he stood there in horror. "Right. Let's go!" In a flash he had passed me and was maneuvering through the crowd toward a back corner of the barn. Since I wasn't in a position to argue, I dashed off after him.

My uncle found the back exit to the barn in no time at all, and he was through it in an instant. As I was closing the door behind us, I saw the hurricane of women spilling into the barn, Aunt Irma in the lead. They were clearing the tables of players, and the barn erupted into a frenzy before my very eyes.

I pulled the door closed and was instantly safe from the commotion. After seeing what was going on inside, the rain hitting me didn't bother me in the least—not anymore.

Uncle Bubba turned around and yelled. "Come on!" through all the chaos. I noticed he was carrying a big platter, which he must have picked up on his way out.

"What've you got?" I hollered over the downpour. I passed my uncle and was leading the way back to my truck.

"Wings, Nephew, wings!" He was high stepping around the huge puddles of water. "I'd fixed a couple of plates to serve to the players tonight. If Irma saw these babies, she'd know I was involved for sure!"

We piled into the cab of my truck, and he put the tray of wings between us. "Let's ride, Nephew!" He pulled back the foil covering, and I saw a couple of varieties that I loved: Hawaiian barbecue, and honey maple hot wings. I inhaled the

succulent aroma. I knew that my rescue would at least provide me with a great late-night snack.

"So where to, Uncle?" I said as I grabbed a honey maple hot wing and bit into it.

"Home, Nephew, home." Uncle Bubba smiled at me. "Hey, the Armadillo business meeting let out early!" My uncle gave me a big wink, and I turned the truck toward his house.

The gamblers didn't get to enjoy the wings, but I certainly did. Thankfully Uncle Bubba wrapped up about half of them for me to take home that night. He probably didn't need them, though. While I was at home enjoying the wings, I'm sure my uncle was busy figuring out a story to tell Aunt Irma about where he really was that night and why his pickup was still parked outside of Junior Newton's barn.

Hawaiian Barbecue Wings

20 chicken wings
¼ cup sugar
2 tsp ginger, ground
1 tsp garlic powder
⅛ cup onions, chopped
¼ tsp white pepper
¼ cup soy sauce
1 Tbsp plum sauce
3 Tbsp honey
¾ cup pineapple juice

Combine all the non-chicken ingredients, then marinate the chicken wings in the mixture overnight—in the refrigerator, of course! To bake them, preheat your oven to 375 degrees. Spread the wings out on a lightly greased cookie sheet. Bake for 45 minutes to an hour, basting with the Hawaiian barbecue marinade occasionally.

Honey Maple Hot Wings

20 chicken wings
1 tsp soy sauce
2 tsp lemon juice
3 Tbsp honey
3 Tbsp regular maple syrup
1 tsp cumin
1 tsp cayenne pepper

Mix all the ingredients together, except for the chicken wings. Preheat oven to 375 degrees, and coat a cookie sheet with a vegetable spray. As you put each wing on the sheet, dip it in the honey-maple mixture. Bake the wings for 15 minutes, then take them out and coat each wing again. Bake another 15 minutes, then take them out and coat them a final time. Bake another 15 minutes or until done.

These also work well on the grill. Just brush with the honey-maple mixture a little more frequently.

Patterson's Grand Finale

Mr. Patterson died on a rainy September Saturday. Uncle Bubba was there with him, and so was Mr. Underwood from the hardware store.

My uncle told me that Mr. Patterson had been in a lot of pain those last few days, and when he finally passed, he did it with a long, restful sigh.

The fellows from the Armadillo Lodge took turns sitting up with the body around the clock over at the Findlebux Funeral Home, which was almost a half-hour away over in the city. I'd always thought it was a creepy place, with heavy maroon curtains trimmed in gold and a nondescript chapel that could be quickly configured to handle whatever kind of religious service the dear departed required.

Uncle Bubba didn't participate in any of those activities, but not because he didn't think a lot of Mr. Patterson. The reason was that my uncle looked at death a lot differently than most people. He figured when he died he was going to make his way up to heaven, and the body he left behind wasn't any different from the hair the barber swept away when he was done with it or the toenails that went flying across the front porch every Saturday morning when he sat out there and clipped them. He had often told Aunt Irma that when he died she should put his body in a cardboard box and set it out front on trash day. No matter how many times he said that, she'd always act shocked that a human could even utter such words.

Uncle Bubba was asked to be a pallbearer, but he declined that role as well. I was sure he would go to the funeral just to show everyone that he cared about Mr. Patterson, but that was probably going to be the extent of it.

I went looking for him on Sunday afternoon. I hadn't spoken to him since the previous day, and I wanted to make sure he was all right. I'd already called his house, and Aunt Irma said she didn't know where he'd gone. After driving around for a few minutes, it hit me. I pointed my pickup out towards Bartdale Creek.

Sure enough, I saw his truck parked there at his favorite fishing hole. He was standing out by the creek. The rain was still coming down strong, but Uncle Bubba was oblivious to it all. The water was dripping off his gimmie cap. I could see that he hadn't brought his fishing gear; instead, he seemed to be just watching the water flow by.

I rolled down the window. "Uncle Bubba? You okay?"

He looked around at me, smiled, and nodded his head. "Yeah, Nephew, I'm fine. How 'bout yourself?"

As I opened the door and walked over to him, I sensed something very melancholy. His eyes were sad, but he grinned as I approached. "So, what are you doing out here, Uncle?"

He kind of chuckled, then just stared out at the creek for a minute. He finally turned back to me. "Well, I've been down here talking to Patterson. If you'd gotten here five minutes earlier, you would have heard me cussin' him a blue streak. Goin' and dying when he did." Uncle Bubba quickly wiped his eye. "Hell, we already had a few shenanigans planned for Halloween."

I couldn't help but smile at my uncle's words. He'd apparently been paying his own personal tribute to Mr. Patterson out here by the creek. "So, do you think he heard you?"

Uncle Bubba shrugged his shoulders and smiled. "I doubt it. He died yesterday, so he's still getting used to whatever it is that heaven's like. Way too busy to listen to me, rambling on down here."

"Maybe not." I put my hand on Uncle Bubba's shoulder. "Mr. Patterson could be up there, getting ready to pull the biggest prank of his life." I clapped him on the back once, then started toward my pickup. I couldn't help but stop, turn around, and offer a final word. "In fact, if I were you, I'd be careful. Patterson's playing with a much bigger deck than you are, now."

Uncle Bubba burst out laughing and waved at me as I left. I felt pretty good about him as I drove away. My uncle was going to be just fine.

Mr. Patterson's funeral was on Monday, and the cement plant let everyone off who wanted to attend. That's the best thing about the company—it was truly a community operation. The weather wasn't cooperating, though; the rain was still pouring and the sky was getting darker.

A large, green canvas covering sporting the dignified lettering *Findlebux Funeral Home* had been erected over the grave, and everyone who could possibly fit was huddled underneath. Many more people from the plant skirted it, as did I, and the umbrellas seemed to form a continuous roof over those mourners. All the Armadillos were there, and I kept waiting to see someone giving the secret sign. No one did, and I was especially glad that I wasn't put under the obligation to reciprocate.

The rain had been collecting in the low points in the cemetery, and many of these small lakes had joined to form a little river that was twisting and turning through the trees and around the tombstones. The weather was getting nasty.

Uncle Bubba was standing a short distance away from the tent. He was wearing his jeans and a denim shirt, which some may have thought inappropriate. I knew better, though. I knew that he'd already said his good-byes to Mr. Patterson down at the creek yesterday.

Pastor Frawley was standing at the end of the grave, and he cleared his throat to indicate that the hearse was approaching. The people grew respectfully quiet, and the six pallbearers from his crew at the cement plant stepped forward. There was no way they could carry the silver casket and their umbrellas, so the men stepped out into the rain and waited for the funeral director to open the large back door of the vehicle.

They carefully slid the casket out, each taking hold of the handles as the box emerged, and began to walk it slowly and somberly toward the grave. The only sound was the rain pouring down.

A huge clap of thunder sounded just as the first two pallbearers walked under the protection of the tent. It startled everyone. Aunt Irma was standing near the grave with Mrs. Mable Matheson, Mrs. Oralee Franklin, and the rest of the Book of Ruth Bible class. They were in charge of the flowers for all of the funerals in the church, and since Mr. Patterson didn't have any family, they had filled the front seats by the grave opening.

The ladies all jumped at the sudden boom, as did the first pallbearer who was unfortunately closest to the grave. He landed with one foot turned out just a little too far, and he lost his footing. The unfortunate man slipped just enough to land next to the coffin-sized opening in the ground. His brow crinkled, his eyes grew wide, and his mouth poised to scream as he continued to slide on the wet grass toward the grave. With a loud cry, he plopped fanny-first into the hole.

This set off a chain of events that I would have never believed if I hadn't been there to witness it myself. Mr. Patterson's silver coffin, short one support person, dipped and bobbed as the other pallbearers struggled for balance.

It was simply too much for the other lead pallbearer. The ground was wet enough that his feet slipped out from under him, and after a hapless struggle, he was propelled toward the grave as well. In desperation he grabbed out for any hold and found Mrs. Franklin's dress. She squealed in fright as she was dragged into the hole with him, screaming and waving her arms wildly.

This was much more than the ladies of the Book of Ruth Bible class could handle, and they gave a simultaneous gasp of horror.

It wasn't over, though. Not by a long shot. With the loss of both of the fellows in front, the others were fighting a losing battle. Mr. Patterson's coffin was swinging in a wide arc as they struggled to regain control. It caught Mrs. Trickle in the side, tapping her with just enough energy to spin her around and send her in a nosedive down into the hole with the others.

The two pallbearers who were already inside had been doing their best to recover from their spill and were on the very verge of getting back their composure when Marianne Trickle came barreling down on them like a cruise missile. She was shrieking in horror, causing them to scream as well.

The good banker was standing next to me, and as his wife disappeared over the edge, he cried out, "Oh Lord, Marianne, hang on! I'm coming to save you, baby!"

He charged forward—an unwise move on the slick grass. A few yards from the hole, he tripped and hit the ground in a belly flop. The momentum kept him going strong. He'd forgotten all about the Mrs. at that point and was wailing like a newborn infant. He slid smoothly in.

Pandemonium swept through the crowd. I was proud of Aunt Irma. Even though her face was locked in a mask of horror and shock, she was doing her best to hold up Mrs. Matheson, who had fallen over in a dead faint somewhere in the course of events.

The remaining pallbearers finally dropped the casket in desperation, fighting to keep themselves prone. One by one, they succumbed to the forces of gravity and motion, and fell to the ground in a tangle of arms and legs.

One of them must have feared sharing the fate of the first two, because he grabbed a corner pole of the tent as he went down, collapsing the entire structure onto the heads of the mourners. The people on the fringes scattered, but I had to just stand and watch—there was something surreal about the whole picture.

The green tent had been transformed into a writhing monstrosity as the people underneath it tried to escape. In the middle of all the screaming and panic, my uncle began to chuckle. It was only a little at first, but as the confusion grew, so did his laughter.

The coffin peeked out underneath one end where the ground was gently sloping. Slowly, lazily, it began to slide. Before long it had moved away from the tent and slipped into the rivulet that had been created by the downpour. The last time I saw Mr. Patterson's casket, it was making its way toward Memorial Avenue, with a few of the funeral home people in hot pursuit.

Uncle Bubba came over to me, and he was laughing so hard that tears were streaming down his face. "Did you see that, Nephew?" He cackled again. "Old man Patterson's alive and well, pulling a final big one on the people of Cut Plug." He turned up his collar. "Well, I'd better go check on Irma."

I looked back, and the confusion was just starting to abate. The tent had been pulled back, and my aunt was standing with some of the other Book of Ruth Bible class ladies, looking down into the grave. "She looks fine, Uncle. In fact, I think they're just getting ready to fish Mrs. Trickle out of the hole."

"Well, shoot. That's not worth stayin' around for." He turned to change course for his truck. "C'mon there, Nephew! I've got some wings cooked at the house!"

He left in a fast trot, and I took out after him. The entire way I heard pieces of some other conversation that he was having—words like "you pulled a good'un" and "dang I wish I could've been in on this."

We got back to his house, and as he pulled some of his wonderful honey cinnamon wings out of the oven, it occurred to me that I hadn't seen my uncle this happy in a long time. I guess it's those unexpected affirmations of faith that mean the most.

We sat there at the kitchen table downing the cinnamon wings at a ferocious pace. Uncle Bubba suddenly looked up and snapped his fingers. "Dang, I almost forgot! I'll be right back!" He disappeared down the hallway and came back in a minute carrying a cardboard box that was just a little larger than a shoe box. "Here." He sat it on the table beside my plate. "This is for you."

I wiped my hands and opened it carefully. I peered in, and a tear welled up at the corner of my eye. Inside the box, sitting majestically in a nest of tissue paper, was an armadillo hat. I lifted it out, and as gaudy and odd as that thing was, I was a little touched. "Mr. Patterson's?"

Uncle Bubba smiled and nodded. "Once he realized that he probably wouldn't be needing it anymore, he made me promise that I'd go get it out of his house. I was supposed to save it until he passed on, then give it to you. He figured it would be an honor for his hat to see in the next generation of Armadillos."

Before this moment, I'd sworn that I would never wear such a contraption. I lifted it to my head, though, and proudly donned the symbol of the Honorable Order of the Armadillo. "I love it," was all I could say. I didn't, of course, but I knew that when I put it on at every meeting, I'd think of Mr. Patterson.

Uncle Bubba frowned. "What're you doing, Nephew?" He hurriedly glanced around the room. "Hide that thing before Irma gets home. You won't make old Patterson happy at all if you start giving our lodge secrets away!"

I just laughed and dug into those wonderful wings.

Honey Cinnamon Wings

20 chicken wings
2 cloves garlic, chopped
¼ cup cooking oil
2 Tbsp soy sauce
¼ cup rice vinegar
¼ cup mild honey
1½ tsp cinnamon
½ tsp thyme
½ tsp ginger
½ tsp dry mustard

Mix all of the ingredients together in a bowl, then add the wings. Refrigerate for a few hours, mixing them around occasionally.

These are wonderful whether you cook them in your oven or on the grill. For the oven, bake them at 375 degrees about 45 minutes, basting with marinade every 10 minutes. On the grill, baste them continually as they cook. In either case, you're going to find that these are wonderful wings.

20

A Proper Dinner Party

When the phone rang on Tuesday evening, I had a gut feeling it was Uncle Bubba. Cut Plug wasn't modernized yet, so we didn't have the fancy Caller ID that I had seen on the television, but I still knew it was him.

"Nephew, you just gotta come over for supper on Friday. Irma's playing cupid for Skeeter and that Effie Marie girl, and you can't make me face that alone!"

I didn't understand at all. I had figured that my aunt would be taking Skeeter's case, since he had made such a mess of it himself, but it didn't sound like that much of a chore. "What are you talking about, Uncle? It sounds like a simple dinner party to me."

"No, you don't get it." There was exasperation in his voice. "Irma's insisting that we all dress up and put on our best manners and show Skeeter's girl how to behave in polite society."

"So what makes you think she doesn't already know?"

"Nephew, she drives a truck, for cryin' out loud! So anyway, Irma's told me to fix up some international wings to make this a more fancy affair."

Now that really was interesting. I loved it when my uncle delved into specialty dishes like that. "What kind of international wings are you going to make, Uncle Bubba?"

He paused for a second. "Well, I'm not quite sure right now. By the time Friday night gets here, though, I'll have something whipped up. We'll see you at suppertime." He hung up the phone, and although this sounded a little on the odd side, I figured I would do anything to help Skeeter out.

I pulled into their driveway on Friday evening, and Skeeter's truck was the only other vehicle there. Effie Marie obviously hadn't arrived yet.

A spicy symphony of scents greeted me on the front porch; I opened the door and went inside. No one was in the living room, so I figured everyone was in the kitchen. "Wow, Uncle Bubba," I called out, "what're you cooking in there?"

"Come on back!" There was a jolly ring to his voice, and I immediately knew he was having fun. "I've got some Italian wings, a recipe from Indonesia, some spicy ones from Jamaica, and even something from Seoul, Korea." By the time he finished running down the evening's menu, I had made it to the kitchen, where I was bathed in the smells of dinner.

Bubba grinned, pulling a pan of wings out of the oven. "How are you doing, boy?"

"Oh, 'bout right." I nodded at my aunt, who was sitting at the table arranging a salad in a large, frosted bowl. Skeeter was sitting next to her, wearing a suit and even a clean white gimmie cap. He was wringing his hands, fidgeting, and looking down at the table. He appeared to be as nervous as I've ever seen him. "How are you, Aunt Irma? Skeeter?"

She nodded and smiled. "Just fine!" She dried off her hand, smiled, and patted Skeeter on the shoulder. "And Skeeter here's going to do marvelously tonight, aren't you?"

He just rapidly nodded his head, his gaze remaining frozen on the tabletop. I looked over at Uncle Bubba, then motioned my head toward the door. We casually drifted into the living room.

"Uncle Bubba, what the heck's wrong with Skeeter? I've never seen him like this!" That much was an absolute fact. He was tied up like the winning knot at a Boy Scout jamboree. If

Effie Marie saw him like this, she was going to be scared clean away.

My uncle just shook his head. "You know Skeeter. First of all, he's always been skittish around women, even back in high school. He's also a little worried that Irma's not going to approve of this girl, no matter how much she tries to convince him otherwise." He glanced back toward the kitchen carefully, then lowered his voice. "We all know this is going to be one rough-cut of a woman, but I think that between you, me, and Irma we'll be able to get some manners into her."

I started to protest the fact that he was making those assumptions without even knowing her but decided my time would be better spent back in the kitchen trying to calm Skeeter down. I had to at least ask the obvious, though. "So, does Effie Marie know that she's coming over here as Skeeter's date?"

"Well of course she does, Nephew! He's the one who invited her over! Anyway, when he got here and saw that Irma had set out the fancy china and our wedding silver, he started worrying that he'd never figure out the order to use the eating utensils." Uncle Bubba shook his head. "Kept going on and on about how he was going to look the fool in front of that Effie woman." He shot another glance toward the kitchen, then chuckled. "Heck, I told him there was no way a truck drivin' gal would be able to resist a city fellow like him, no matter which fork he ate with!" He slapped me on the back, then headed back toward the kitchen. "C'mon, Nephew!"

While my uncle tended to the wings, I sat down in the chair across the table from Skeeter. "Lookin' good, bud."

The only acknowledgement I got was a slight movement of his head up and down.

"He sure is," Aunt Irma reassured. "Now Skeeter, you just sit here and talk to Nephew while I check on the table one more time." She leaned over and straightened his collar, then left the table for the dining room.

"Just relax now, Skeeter. Things are going to be just fine." I leaned across the table, and bent down so I could look him in his eyes. "This is going to be a great evening."

He slowly looked up and had just started to speak, when the tinkling sound of the doorbell suddenly echoed through the house. Skeeter froze.

Aunt Irma's face appeared in the kitchen doorway. "Skeeter, would you like to answer the door?" When he didn't move, my aunt marched into the kitchen and took him by the elbow. In a single, sweeping movement, she had pulled him from the chair and was ushering him toward the front door.

Uncle Bubba came sauntering in and pulled the pan containing the wings out of the oven. He examined them closely, ever the critical cook. They must have passed his scrutiny, because my uncle nodded his head and began to transfer them to a serving platter. As he did, he looked back over his shoulder and grinned. "I'll tell you what, Nephew, this is going to be one special dinner. I put the fix in for Skeeter earlier while Irma was setting the table."

That immediately caught my attention. "What kind of fix are you talking about, Uncle Bubba?" I could only hope that my uncle was leaving the matchmaking up to Aunt Irma. She at least had some experience with such matters.

"Let's just say that I'm orchestrating the evening for him." Uncle Bubba smiled, then winked at me. "See, when I figure the time's right, I'm going to give Skeeter the secret signal," he stopped and placed his hand over his mouth, just like he was yawning. "When he sees this, he knows it's time to start reciting his love poem to Effie Marie."

That tactic certainly hadn't worked well the first time he tried to impress her with his poetic ability, and I was pretty sure he should just let it lay at this point. I was just about to mention that to my uncle, when Aunt Irma burst back into the room.

"Well, gentlemen, we have company!" She was positively beaming. I wasn't prepared for what happened next. Effie Marie Callahan stepped into the kitchen, looking more beautiful than I could have possibly imagined. She was wearing a bright blue dress, modestly cut above the knee, but it still revealed a dynamite figure. Her brown hair, which was usually tucked up under a gimmie cap, was long and flowing over her shoulders.

"You're Effie?" my uncle said, a look of shock on his face. As usual, Uncle Bubba's mouth was on automatic pilot. Aunt Irma shot him a cutting glance, and he quickly extended his hand to his guest. "I mean, we haven't officially met, even though I've seen you around the plant."

Effie Marie took his hand daintily and gave it a small shake. "It is a genuine pleasure to meet you, Bubba. I've certainly heard all the legends of your prowess with chicken wings."

"Uh, yeah." He stood there staring at her. My uncle was apparently dumbfounded by the metamorphosis from the truck driver that we had all seen.

Aunt Irma quickly picked up the slack. "And this is our nephew, who works out at the plant as well."

Effie shook my hand with the same poise as she had Uncle Bubba's. "Very nice to meet you!"

"And nice to meet you, too, Effie." For the first time since she'd entered the room, I noticed Skeeter. He was standing there like he was in a trance. It wasn't hard to figure out that he was mesmerized by her beauty. I had to agree, it was certainly a change from her everyday appearance.

Aunt Irma took the salad bowl from the kitchen table, then hurried off toward the dining room. "Come on, everyone, let's sit down to dinner." We followed her in a procession, with Uncle Bubba bringing up the rear. He carried the platter of wings triumphantly.

We took our places at the table, Bubba on one end and me on the other. Aunt Irma sat to his right, with Skeeter and Effie Marie across from her.

Effie carefully unfolded her napkin and spread it out in her lap. Neither Uncle Bubba nor Skeeter had ever eaten a meal with their napkin in their lap, but tonight they both scrambled to follow Effie Marie's lead.

Aunt Irma picked up the bowl of salad and passed it across the table to Skeeter. "You two go ahead and help yourselves first."

Skeeter took the bowl and looked a little confused. Effie leaned over and quietly said, "You might want to use the smaller plate that is sitting in the big one." She smiled and pointed to the setting in front of him.

My aunt nodded as Skeeter started heaping the salad onto his plate, letting him know that he was doing well. "So, Effie Marie, why don't you tell us all about yourself?" I could sense that Aunt Irma was using one of her quiet methods of prying information out of a person. She offered a basket of bread to the guest. "I heard that you've only been in town for a few months."

She smiled and shrugged. "Oh, there's not much to tell, really. I wanted to get a simple job in a small, docile town, and since I owned stock in the cement plant I thought it might be the perfect place to start."

My interest piqued immediately. "Stock?" No one had stock in the plant—it was privately held.

"Oh, I guess you didn't know. My great uncle was one of the founders of the cement plant. Over the years, most family members have been given small pieces here and there." She stopped and glanced downward, like she was suddenly embarrassed. "I never really thought about it, until last year."

For the first time, at least that I had heard, Skeeter spoke. "Well, what happened a year ago, Effie?"

She sighed. "Long story, short. I graduated from Texas A&M more years ago than I care to divulge, and I landed a job as an accountant for a New York firm. Through the years I worked my way up to a senior accounting position."

"Dang, Effie!" Skeeter definitely sounded impressed. "That's great!"

"Well, one might think. I was working fifteen-hour days, seven days a week, though. I never had time to even go on a date, and if I dared to think about any personal time, the company frowned on it severely. My only friends were in the office, and we were constantly at each others' throats from the pressure." She stopped to take a small bite of salad. "Two of my colleagues were arguing over a schedule during a meeting, and one of them had a stroke right there before our very eyes. He was gone before his head even hit the table. It was then I decided that a simpler life might be a better quality life, and I remembered the plant my great uncle had founded in a small town in Texas. The only job open that week was driving one of the trucks, and the rest is history." She looked around the table, and I'm not sure I'd ever seen anyone happier. "Since then, my blood pressure is down twenty points, I can sleep through the night without a single worry, and I've been meeting all sorts of wonderful people. Tonight, I'm thankful to have increased that number even more!"

Uncle Bubba quickly stood up. "Nephew, where in the world did you put that seasoning for the wings. Come on in the kitchen and help me find it!" He walked around the table, grabbed my arm, and practically dragged me out of the room.

"Uncle Bubba, what in the world are you doing?" My elbow was hurting, so I pulled it away from him. "And what seasoning are you talking about; you're always angry when people add things to your wings!"

He shushed me and peeked back in the dining room. "Nephew," he whispered, "we've got a real problem here. This woman is an honest-to-goodness sophisticated lady. We can't let Skeeter stand up and start reciting that crazy poem of his!"

If there was anything that scared me more than one of my uncle's hair-brained plans, it was when he started changing one of those schemes on the fly. "Uncle Bubba, I was afraid of this from the first time I heard everyone assuming that Effie Marie was some kind of country bumpkin just because she was a woman who drove a truck. The answer is simple, though: Just don't give Skeeter the signal."

Uncle Bubba's eyes lit up. "You know, you're right! C'mon, let's get back in there!"

I put my hand out to stop him. "Look, you'd at least better go back in there with the seasoning that we supposedly came in here to find."

He snapped his fingers, then grabbed the salt and pepper off the kitchen table. "Well, all right then!" He stalked out of the room, so I followed him back in.

Aunt Irma was in the middle of a thought when we walked in. "So I know that the other members of the Cut Plug Garden Club would just love to meet you, Effie."

She then launched into a detailed explanation of the activities of the garden club, complete with the yearly activity schedule, contests, and so forth. It had taken fifteen minutes for Aunt Irma to just get to summer, so I knew this was going to be the long part of the evening. Everyone had been eating as we listened, but the meal had slowed considerably until we were all sitting around the table focused on my aunt. Skeeter was starting to fade, his eyes drooping, and he was unable to suppress a massive yawn.

Uncle Bubba did the same thing, and I saw him slowly cover his mouth with his hand as he did. I suddenly realized what was going on. Uncle Bubba was unknowingly giving the sign to Skeeter.

It wasn't lost on him, either. Skeeter suddenly sprang to life. He jumped up out of his chair, in the middle of Aunt Irma's explanation of how garden club merit points were earned throughout the year. He cleared his throat and began to recite. "Effie, oh Effie, you make my heart beat."

Uncle Bubba cleared his throat and began to shake his head slightly in a negative gesture. He was obviously trying to get Skeeter to stop before any damage was done.

Aunt Irma resented the interruption, though, and I saw her narrow her eyes at my uncle. There was a muffled thump under the table—she'd kicked him a good one.

Skeeter finished reciting his poem as we all sat there in rapt attention, and when he finally concluded, Aunt Irma began to clap. Uncle Bubba and I joined in, and Effie Marie was blushing crimson.

She finally spoke up. "Skeeter, I can't say that I've ever been so complimented. You are quite the articulate poet—and a bit of a romantic, I might add." Her eyes locked with his, and something special passed between them.

Uncle Bubba broke the silence. "Nephew, everyone seems to be done. Help me get some of these plates into the kitchen." We gathered up what we could and placed them carefully in the kitchen sink. He turned the water on to let them soak and took a deep breath. "You know, I think everything may have worked out just fine."

I couldn't help but laugh. "Maybe so, Uncle Bubba, maybe so."

He glanced over at me, then paused for a second. "C'mon." He opened the door that led outside from the kitchen and stepped out into the evening. "Things are starting to wind down. Let's go out to the garage and have a sip of Tennessee bourbon to celebrate."

I followed him outside, and by the time he'd poured us a little bit in a couple of mason jars, things were settling down in the house. I stood in the garage, looking back. I could see Aunt Irma starting to clean up in the kitchen, and out in front of the house, Skeeter and Effie were settling into the porch swing.

Uncle Bubba poured a little more into my jar, and I stood there assessing life for a moment. I was happy, which was more than most people could boast. Uncle Bubba didn't have his restaurant, but he and Aunt Irma were wearing their middle age well. And Skeeter—well, I could see that he had settled down and was letting Effie Marie see the real fellow that everyone knew. While I was watching them in the swing, I saw him slowly slide his arm around her shoulders, just like they were a couple of high school kids sparking on the front porch.

I heaved a great sigh. On this night in Cut Plug, Texas, things were right with the world.

Italian Dressing Wings

20 chicken wings
¼ cup of your favorite hot sauce
½ cup Italian salad dressing (regular or fat free)
½ tsp salt
½ tsp black pepper
¼ tsp red pepper
¼ tsp garlic powder

Bake the wings in the oven at 375 degrees for about 45 minutes or until done. While they're cooking, mix all the other ingredients together in a bowl. Remove the wings from the oven and dip each one in the mixture. Allow them to stand for about 10 minutes, and they're ready to serve!

Indonesian Wings

20 chicken wings
1 stick of butter
¼ cup soy sauce
1 tsp ground coriander
2 Tbsp lime juice

Start by melting the butter in a pan, then adding the soy sauce, coriander, and lime juice. Mix well, then add the chicken wings and place them in the fridge. They will need to marinate for at least a couple of hours. Overnight is even better.

Even though Uncle Bubba fixed them in the oven on the night of the big date, these are just as delicious when they're grilled. Bake them for 45 minutes, or grill them until they are done. In either case, stop and baste them occasionally in the process.

Jamaican Style Wings

20 chicken wings
4 fresh jalapeno peppers, seeded and chopped
1 cup minced onion
4 green onions, chopped
4 garlic cloves, chopped
¼ tsp nutmeg
½ tsp cinnamon
½ tsp thyme
1 tsp salt
1 tsp sugar
1 tsp allspice
2 tsp black pepper
2 Tbsp soy sauce
¼ cup olive oil
1 Tbsp white vinegar

Combine all the remaining ingredients, except the chicken wings, in a blender. Puree until a thick paste forms. In the world of Jamaican cooking, this result is known as jerk paste. Put the jerk paste into a bowl, then add the chicken wings and toss until the wings are well coated. Cover the bowl with foil and refrigerate overnight.

These wings are best prepared in the oven, so begin by preheating to 375 degrees. Arrange the wings on a greased cookie sheet and bake for approximately 45 minutes. If you brush the wings with some of the residual jerk paste while they're cooking, it will add to the flavor immensely!

Korean Wings

20 chicken wings
3 Tbsp soy sauce
4 Tbsp dry sherry
2 Tbsp sugar
2 minced garlic cloves
2 tsp ginger
2 tsp sesame seeds
2 Tbsp sesame oil
½ tsp pepper

Mix all ingredients together in a bowl, and marinate the wings for at least two hours. This is another example of Uncle Bubba's recipes that translates just as well from the oven to the grill. Just like the Indonesian wings, bake these at 375 degrees for about 45 minutes, or put them on the grill once the coals have grayed. If you brush them with marinade occasionally in the process, these wings will be even better!

Grand Theft Wood Tick

J had stopped by Hinkley's Grocery to pick up a loaf of bread and was just getting out of my truck, when Uncle Bubba came roaring into the parking lot.

"Nephew! C'mon and get in here!" He gestured for me toward his pickup.

I pointed toward the store. "I was just going to get some bread, Uncle. What's going on?"

"Got some maple-mustard wings fixed. Way too many for us to eat. You've just got to come help out." He was insistent. "Just leave your truck here in the parking lot. It'll be fine."

It would be, of course. The worst crime spree that Cut Plug had seen was when some folks from Tater Springs came over and stole the mascot off the sign in front of the high school. It was an insult to the mighty Cut Plug Opossums, both the current students and the alumni. The graduating class of 1977 had paid to have the giant opossum put up on the marquee sign, and it was a catastrophe when the town awakened to find that it was gone.

Still, that was a rarity in a town where people seldom locked the doors of their homes, and never those of their cars. With that in mind, I shrugged my shoulders and climbed in the passenger side of his truck.

From the way he was heading, I could tell we weren't going to his house. "Uh, Uncle Bubba." I was a little apprehensive. "I thought we were going to eat some maple-mustard wings. It looks to me like you're heading out of town."

He seemed to weigh my statement for a minute. "Nephew, I've got to tell you something that's top secret. I'm bringing you in on a covert Armadillo mission. Most of the fellows in the lodge don't even know about it, and if we get caught, we can't admit our affiliation."

I put my head in my hands and rubbed my temples to relieve some of the pressure that had just erupted. "You know, Uncle Bubba, I may not be the Armadillo to help you with this."

He waved off my suggestion. "Nonsense. You're the new blood in the lodge, and that makes it perfect." We pulled into a hay pasture that I knew had belonged to Skeeter's dad. After his passing, Skeeter had taken it over and leased it out to one of the local ranchers.

The truck's headlights swept through the field, and I saw that we were approaching a couple of pickup trucks. Skeeter's was there, so was the big double-cab that Mr. Trembley owned, and the rack of deer horns on the front of the other meant that Buck was in attendance as well.

We pulled up to the back of Buck's pickup, where he and Skeeter were huddled around a small, portable grill. I could smell the maple in the wings and hear them popping on the fire. I figured if nothing else, at least I'd get a good meal.

Uncle Bubba took a wing for himself, then handed one to me. "Eat up, Nephew. We've got a lot of work ahead of us."

Mr. Trembley must have just arrived, because he was looking the wings over like he hadn't had one yet. "I think I'll try one, too." He took a bite, and his eyebrows raised. "Dang, Bubba, these are some mighty fine chicken wings! You really ought to open up that chicken wing restaurant you were talking about."

My uncle just shrugged. "If I could only figure out how."

I dug into the drumette, and as always, the wings were great. They were extremely hot from the grill, and I was doing my best to balance between tearing into one and burning my mouth. "So what's all this about, Uncle?"

"It's about honor, Nephew." Uncle Bubba's tone was solemn. "It's all about honor." He nodded toward Skeeter. "Wrap up the rest of the wings, and let's get started."

Skeeter produced a couple of sheets of foil and crafted a makeshift bowl. After he'd transferred all the wings over, Buck doused the fire.

Mr. Trembley pulled out his keys with a jingling of metal. "We oughta take my truck so we can all ride inside."

Buck got in the front seat, and I was stuck in the back seat between Skeeter and my Uncle Bubba. At least those extended cab trucks had a lot of room.

Skeeter was passing around the maple-mustard wings, and I took another one when they came by. "So where are we going?" I asked with a mouth full of maple-mustard and chicken. "And whose honor got defamed?"

My uncle had a stern expression on his face. "Ours did, Nephew, ours did. The whole town of Cut Plug. And word is, it's gonna happen again." There were mumbles of agreement from the others. "This time, though, we're going to beat them to it."

I was completely confused. "I'm sorry, Uncle Bubba, but I don't have a clue as to what you're going on about."

Buck turned around. "It's the folks from Tater Springs—we heard a rumor that they were going to come steal the mascot off of the marquee in front of the high school again." His eyes narrowed. "But we're gonna go get theirs first!"

I got a bad feeling in my gut. "You fellows can't be serious."

Uncle Bubba just nodded his head. "That's right, Nephew. We're gonna steal their team mascot that's on top of their marquee. We're going after the Tater Springs Wood Tick."

"You guys must be crazy!" I knew my voice was raised a little, but I couldn't believe what I was hearing. "Do you know what will happen to us if we get caught? We could get thrown in the county jail!"

Skeeter shook his head. "I don't know, your uncle's got a mighty fine plan!"

"I don't care how good a plan it is, if the Tater Springs police catch us, we're going to be in some serious trouble!" I seemed to be the only one who could rationalize that, though, so the pickup kept going down the road to Tater Springs. I fretted the entire way there.

When we arrived, I learned that Uncle Bubba's big plan was to drive around until we found the town's police cruiser parked for the night. We finally located it at Tater Springs' only late-night hamburger joint, and my uncle pronounced our situation as being safe.

Our next stop was in the parking lot of the Tater Springs High School. The sign out in front proudly proclaimed, "Home of the Fightin' Wood Ticks!" Sure enough, perched on top of the sign, was a giant tick. It looked like it was only slightly smaller than an old Volkswagen Beetle. The bloated mascot was light brown in color and had little black legs sticking out all around it. The front two legs had little boxing gloves on them, presumably to show the aggressive spirit of the school. I couldn't even begin to imagine what could have led the long-ago founders of the school to choose this creature as their mascot.

Still, there it was, and my uncle was aiming to steal it. Mr. Trembley shut off the lights in his truck and drove it around into the shadows at the side of the building.

"Everyone know what to do?" my uncle whispered.

This was crazy. "No! Not only do I have no idea what my job is here, but I think you're all out of your minds for giving this a minute of consideration."

Everyone shushed me at once. "Nephew, all you have to do is help us lift." My uncle patted me on the knee. "And if it makes you feel any better, we'll all swear that you weren't involved if we get caught."

"That's right, son," Mr. Trembley added. "Just give us a hand and we'll make sure you don't get arrested."

Skeeter slipped quietly out of the truck, and I watched him dash across the front lawn of the high school. He squatted down beside each spotlight that lit the sign and quickly unscrewed them.

The only light that remained was the flourescent illumination behind the marquee section of the sign. It was considerably dimmer, though, and might provide the cover that these fellows needed. Trembley slowly pulled the truck out into the open. Uncle Bubba nudged me and we got out, while Trembley eased the vehicle flush against the back side of the sign. Buck and Skeeter produced wrenches, then climbed up onto the side of the truck bed. They leaned over and began to unbolt the monster tick from the marquee sign.

Bubba pulled himself up into the bed of the truck and motioned for me to join him. I looked around quickly, and since there weren't any other cars in sight, I climbed up behind him. We positioned ourselves behind Skeeter and Buck, ready to help with the handoff of the tick.

When it came off, it was with a terrible vengeance. While that gigantic wood tick wasn't any heavier than we'd anticipated, it was certainly more awkward to balance. Had it not been so massive, two or three people could have lifted it easily. Handling it while standing up in the back of a pickup in the dead of night, though, was a different matter. Skeeter and Buck lost their balance almost immediately and shifted it back to us. Uncle Bubba and I did our best to keep the tick above our heads, and it was touch and go for a few minutes. We finally got it stable enough to hold. Skeeter added his support next, and Buck gave it enough stability that we could hold it.

"All right, fellows," Uncle Bubba said with a heavy breath. "Let's ease this thing down into the bed of the truck!"

It actually looked like we were going to pull off the great tick theft, when I heard Mr. Trembley start yelling inside the truck. It took me a minute to make out the words, but I finally did. He was yelling at the top of his voice, "Hang on, boys, it's the police!"

My eyes locked with Uncle Bubba's for a moment, and I could see the look of sheer horror in them. "Oh, Lord!" was all he got out, before the truck began to pull forward.

We all scrambled to steady ourselves in the bed of the truck, with the wood tick held high above our heads. Mr. Trembley was cutting across the schoolyard at an ever-increasing speed. Each little bump and dip gave us a fit, but we somehow managed to keep the creature airborne long enough for the pickup to get back on the highway.

We were actually doing pretty well, when Skeeter finally made a sterling observation. "So, where are these police, anyway?"

We all looked around, and sure enough, we were alone on the road. "I don't know," Uncle Bubba said, "but we seem to be on a roll. Let's just hang on and see if we can get this thing home."

It was the longest ride of my life, standing up in the back of that truck, supporting that horrible thing. We must have really looked a sight, an extended cab pickup driving down the back roads between Tater Springs and Cut Plug with a huge, brown wood tick on its back.

I've never been so relieved as when we bounced back into the pasture. When Mr. Trembley slowed the truck to a stop, we finally eased the giant wood tick down. It completely filled the bed of the truck, with its stubby little legs hanging over the side.

The fellows jumped down and started slapping high fives, and I hadn't seen a more excited bunch of guys since the Cut Plug FFA won best of show for their prize calf at the county fair.

Uncle Bubba and the other covert Armadillos finally calmed down, and Skeeter fetched the remaining chicken wings out of the pickup. We all dug in, hungry after the evening's adventure, I suppose.

As we stood there munching and savoring the maple and mustard flavors, I made what I considered to be an off-hand remark. "So, guys, now that you have the Tater Springs Wood Tick, what are you planning to do with it?"

Everyone suddenly fell silent. I realized that no one had thought that far ahead.

"Well," Uncle Bubba pondered, "I guess we could keep it over at the Armadillo Lodge."

Even I knew what a bad idea that was. "Uncle Bubba, there's just no way Junior's going to let you store this thing in his barn. The last thing in the world he needs is to get into trouble for harboring stolen goods."

My uncle nodded, then looked over to Mr. Trembley. "You know, you've got that big garage of yours out behind your house."

Trembley held up his hands to stop Uncle Bubba before he could finish. "Ain't no way we're putting it in my garage. My wife'd kill you and me both."

Skeeter was looking a little nervous. "Well, we can't just leave it here in the pasture. It'd get traced to me in a heartbeat." He took another wing and concentrated on picking it clean, having said his piece.

There was a long pause before my uncle finally snapped his fingers. "I've got it! This is perfect!" He seemed extremely satisfied with himself. "Everyone eat up; let's finish off these wings and put a wrap on this thing."

We did just that.

I only got a few hours' sleep that night, because Uncle Bubba and I had to be up at the first peep of dawn. I met him at his house and we walked the few blocks over to Mr. Trickle's. More precisely, we hid in the bushes two houses down. The good banker had just gone outside in his robe and pajamas to get the newspaper when Deputy Hernandez came rolling up with Tater Springs' two officers, and both cars had their police lights flashing. That alone surprised Mr. Trickle, but he was shocked even more when they pointed over to his wife's azalea bushes. Hovering directly over them, balanced on two saw horses placed in the bushes, was a giant wood tick.

Uncle Bubba and I watched Mr. Trickle standing there dealing with the police and trying to look dignified in his nightclothes.

All in all, I'd have to give a nod to my uncle on his plan. It was truly a success.

Maple-Mustard Wings

20 chicken wings
3 Tbsp olive oil
2 cloves minced garlic
2 tsp dried rosemary
2 Tbsp balsamic vinegar
$\frac{1}{3}$ cup maple syrup
2 Tbsp Dijon mustard

Mix all ingredients together, and marinate the wings overnight in the refrigerator. Save the marinade mixture to use when cooking.

Uncle Bubba likes these prepared on the grill, but for once, I disagree with his culinary expertise. I like these prepared in the oven much better. For the grill, let the coals go completely to gray. Grill the marinated wings, turning and brushing frequently with the sauce. When the wings are nearly finished, stop applying the marinade and let them cook until done.

To prepare them in the oven, set the temperature to 375 and bake for about 45 minutes on a greased shallow pan. Brush and turn occasionally to ensure even cooking. No matter how you prepare them, though, you're going to find this odd combination of maple and mustard delicious!

The Last Ride of the Giant Armadillo

I'd have bet my house that the day would never come: Uncle Bubba and banker Trickle on the same side of any issue.

The way the whole thing came about was by accident, really. Mr. Trickle happened to hear of a team of investors who wanted to open a hotel in some rural spot in Texas. These folks had visions of conventions and corporate meetings that were far from the bustle of the big city, and as it turns out, it's hard to get further away from anything than in Cut Plug.

The good banker called them up and invited them to town for an inspection tour, just to look the place over. As it turned out, it was also homecoming weekend at the high school, so the football game would be an especially exciting addition to their visit.

Trickle called a special meeting of the city council to tell the rest of the town what was going on and to hopefully win support for the idea. I heard he gave a rousing speech, at least that's what Uncle Bubba said. I was never interested enough in town politics to attend city council meetings. Still, it surprised me to no end that my uncle was behind any idea that Mr. Trickle had.

The new hotel quickly became the main topic of conversation in the cafeteria at the plant, and the townsfolk were pretty much split down the middle on the issue. Some thought the infusion of cash into the Cut Plug economy would be a great thing, while others saw the whole affair as an invasion of the town's privacy. I didn't really have an opinion either way.

In fact, I was pretty removed from all the festivities. I'd heard that Mr. Trickle was taking them on a tour through the town, and that the Cut Plug Garden Club even put on a special slide presentation highlighting the beautiful foliage in the city. I didn't see any of it until I showed up at the homecoming game.

It was a regular carnival there—certainly more than the average football game. Some people had booths set up to sell specialty food items, and others were peddling all kinds of paraphernalia emblazoned with the Cut Plug High School colors of green and blue. I came up on Aunt Irma's biscotti booth, where she seemed to be doing a whiz-bang business rivaled only by Uncle Bubba's wing stand.

My uncle wasn't there, though; Buck was behind the table pushing the wings. I stood in line, and in a only a few minutes I was faced with the decision of selecting apricot wings, lemon herb wings, or even some of my uncle's extravagant pepper mint wings. I took the half-dozen plate of lemon herb and peeled off a few dollars to give Buck.

He was reluctant at first. "Hey, I don't think Bubba would want me to go charging you for wings! Just help yourself." He gestured at the large pans of chicken wings on the table. "Just be sure and tell Bubba that I let you off for free!"

I dropped the money on the table. "Now c'mon, Buck. We both know that my uncle is trying to raise enough money to start his restaurant. That's a cause I'll gladly donate to." I picked up one of the lemon-flavored wings and took a bite. "Besides, food this good is worth the price."

Aunt Irma had watched the exchange, and she stepped around the table. "You sure are a sweet boy," she said and kissed me on the cheek. "If your uncle ever does get his wing place, he'll have you to thank for a lot of it."

I couldn't help but blush. "Aw, Aunt Irma. If Uncle Bubba makes it in the chicken wing business, it'll be due to his talents as a chef." I was surprised that he wasn't at the booth himself, come to think of it. "By the way, Aunt Irma, where is he?"

Buck grinned like a possum, so I knew he had the answer. "Bubba's got something special planned for those city folks who're wanting to build the hotel." He winked at me, and I instantly knew this was one of my uncle's schemes that I should probably be worried about. Since I didn't have the slightest idea what it was, though, I figured I'd just try to enjoy the game without fretting too much about him or what he'd gotten himself into.

The first half of the game was pretty uneventful, with the Tater Springs Wood Ticks stopping us every time we tried to score. We did the same to them, so for the most part, the boys were just out there tearing up the middle of the field.

I saw Mr. Trickle sitting up close to the top of the grandstands with several people in business suits, and I figured this was the hoity-toity delegation that had caused all the buzz in town. They seemed to be enjoying themselves. Mr. Trickle was laughing and talking with them and pointing out first one thing and then another.

Halftime was approaching, and the marching bands were starting to line up along the sidelines for their big mid-game performance. As was customary, the visiting team's band would march first, and then the Mighty Cut Plug Fighting Opossum Band would take the field. It was quite a name for the twenty-three-member band, but Francis Carpell, the band director, insisted that it added a mystique to the group that would entice other students to join. It was a scheme that didn't seem to be working, sadly.

Nevertheless, I watched them taking their positions right behind the players' bench. It was hard not to get caught up in the pageantry. The players were giving their all on the field in the last few minutes of the half; the bands were lined up in their colorful uniforms; the cheerleaders were bouncing along the track in front of the grandstand; and the whole scene was punctuated by the smell of fresh popcorn in the air. Right about then, something caught my eye.

At the far end of the field, some huge, gray object was invading the track. In horror, I realized it was Uncle Bubba's giant armadillo.

I'm not sure whether he was promoting the Armadillo Lodge or just trying to add to the fanfare, but the monstrosity began to creep down the track that ran around the football field. The armadillo was coming our way, a chicken wing in one claw and the school flag in the other. From the small hole in the top, I could see Skeeter's head peeking through. The maneuvering mechanism had apparently been unimproved since the giant armadillo last saw the light of day.

The beast was gaining speed, and I assumed that Uncle Bubba merely wanted to do a pass-by of the grandstands. It had caught the attention of the crowd by then, and all the hustle and bustle of the game had come to a dead halt. The final play of the game stopped without any fanfare. Every eye in the stadium was locked on the armadillo.

Uncle Bubba had the thing moving at a pretty good clip by the time it was even with the goal line, and he was heading for the fifty. The kids were certainly getting a big kick out of it. The band members were laughing and shouting as it approached, waving at it like it was a real animal and not a contraption made of chicken wire and plaster.

Skeeter was staring straight ahead and was presumably giving the appropriate signals by pounding on the top of the cab of Uncle Bubba's pickup.

They were about even with the thirty-yard line, and the crowd was going wild. Skeeter glanced over, and his face froze in an expression of awe and wonder. I followed his gaze and saw that Effie Marie Callahan was sitting just a few rows below me. A grin split Skeeter's face, and he started hollering, "Effie! Effie, look here!" His head was bobbing up and down like he was jumping in the bed of the truck, somewhere in the innards of the giant armadillo.

Effie Marie waved at him and yelled, "Skeeter! Hi, Skeeter!"

That's all it took. Skeeter forced his hand through the top of the armadillo so he could wave at Effie. I'm not sure what was going on inside, though, because the beast was starting to sway something fierce.

I wanted to call out to Uncle Bubba, but I knew he was driving blind. It was clear to me that Skeeter was completely focused on Effie Marie at the moment, and I saw absolutely no way I could help my uncle.

I don't know what bizarre instructions Skeeter was sending to Uncle Bubba, but the giant armadillo was starting to careen out of control. The excitement in the eyes of the band students quickly changed to panic as the huge creature turned their way, heading for the bench at the fifty-yard line.

The band members scattered, tossing their instruments in the air as they scrambled for safety. The crowd that had been clapping wildly had stopped in a collective gasp of horror.

With a combination of the band and football team running before it, the armadillo headed for the center of the field. The students' arms were flailing, and they were all screaming with cries of fear and terror.

Uncle Bubba must have noticed that his plan had gone terribly wrong, because the truck stopped abruptly. My uncle apparently slammed on the brakes, but the shell of the armadillo around it kept moving. It was launched a good twenty yards away from the truck, with Skeeter riding it down. His eyes had suddenly gotten as wide as moon pies, and he was screeching like a banshee.

It hit in midfield, showering two-by-fours and chunks of plaster in every direction. The giant armadillo was disintegrating before our eyes.

I jumped up and ran for the field, hoping Skeeter wasn't hurt. There was a slight delay when I stopped to climb over the four-foot fence that separated the track from the grandstand, but Effie Marie leapt over the fence like a hurdler and continued toward the remains of the armadillo in a dead run.

"Skeeter!" She was yelling at the top of her lungs. "Skeeter, are you okay?" I saw that her eyes were filled with tears as she passed me.

On the football field, pieces of the armadillo began to fall away as a single hand broke through the pile, fighting for freedom. A moment later Skeeter's head popped up, and as soon as he saw Effie Marie, he squirted up out of the debris like he'd been smeared with lard.

"Effie!" He dashed past Uncle Bubba's pickup and toward the grandstand. Suddenly, everything seemed to move in slow motion. It was like one of those old black-and-white movies, where the hero and heroine ran slowly across a grassy field toward each other. Effie Marie and Skeeter were covering ground in long leaps.

When they finally met, it was a beautiful moment. Their arms intertwined and their lips met. I'm sure every lady in the stadium that night felt a wave of emotion watching those two.

I kept going until I caught up with Uncle Bubba. He was standing at the edge of the debris pile that used to be his giant armadillo. "You okay?" I asked.

He just shook his head slowly from side to side. "Dang that Skeeter." He shot a hard glance back over his shoulder at the lovebirds. "He was supposed to be helping me navigate around the track." Uncle Bubba shook his head again and then walked away. I could tell that my uncle was more than a little angry.

I figured that he needed a few minutes alone, so I walked back off the field. Instead of taking my seat again, I headed for the table where Buck was still moving those wonderful wings.

On the way past the stands, I could see that the hotel delegation was standing there in shock, their mouths hanging open and their gazes locked onto the playing field. Banker Trickle was talking fast, and although I couldn't hear what he was saying, I could see that he was desperately trying to convince them that Cut Plug was a stable community.

I couldn't help but laugh out loud. I walked up to Buck in the wing stand, and he knew something was up. "What the heck's goin' on out there? You should have heard all the commotion from back here!"

I just smiled. "I'll let my uncle give you the details. Meanwhile, fix me up another helping of wings."

They were mighty good that night, and the variety made the booth a big hit. Feel free to try them on your own, whether it's for sale at your own booth at homecoming, or just for a few friends at the house. All three recipes are prepared exactly the same way, which helps out if you want to have some variety the next time you're making chicken wings!

Pepper Mint Wings

20 chicken wings
1 16-oz. can whole tomatoes, rinsed and drained
¼ cup olive oil
1 whole jalapeño, chopped fine
1 clove garlic, chopped fine
20 whole mint leaves, chopped
½ cup water

This one sounds pretty strange, but Uncle Bubba swears by it! When you serve them, people certainly take notice. Most folks hear the name and think of pepper-mint, but these wings have more of an Italian taste. They're prepared the same way as the other two recipes in this chapter.

Apricot Wings

20 chicken wings
1 bottle dark beer
1 package dried apricots
1 Tbsp onion flakes
2 tsp minced garlic
1 tsp ginger
1 tsp cinnamon
½ tsp salt
½ tsp white pepper

The apricot wings have an unusual flavor, kind of tart, a little sweet, just like an apricot! It's a subtle flavor, though, and the juicy taste of the chicken wing still comes through. Use the instructions for the lemon herb wings to prepare them.

Lemon Herb Wings

20 chicken wings
2 tsp rosemary
2 tsp minced garlic
½ tsp white pepper
½ tsp salt
½ cup lemon juice
½ cup olive oil

These recipes require no marinating, so they're perfect to fix on the fly. They are also unique dishes—ones that your guests will talk about. They were certainly a big hit at the homecoming game! Start by preheating your oven to 375 degrees. Put all of the ingredients into a baking pan, stirring the mixture well. The wings need to bake for at least 45 minutes, but start checking them after about 30 to make sure they don't overcook. Of course, if you're preparing all three, just use separate dishes!

The Great Thanksgiving Turkey Hunt

One of the main social centers of Cut Plug was the cafeteria at the cement plant. Employees gathered there before work for coffee, when they were on breaks, and especially at lunch.

It was exactly one week before Thanksgiving, and on that particular day I had gone through the food line and picked up a hearty helping of chopped ham. I was trying to decide whether to sit down with some of the folks inside or go out and eat at one of the picnic tables on the adjoining patio. Buck made the decision for me when he grabbed my elbow and steered me through the doors that led outside.

He pointed me at a table that was vacant, with the exception of a tray of food that I assumed to be his. I sat, and Buck plopped down on the bench across from me. He took off his gimmie cap and sighed. "You know we've got a problem with your uncle, don't you?"

The way things had been going, it could have been anything. I didn't even hazard a guess. "What've you got, Buck?"

"Well, it's Bubba and Skeeter. Those two haven't spoken a word since homecoming." The big man frowned and slowly stirred a helping of mashed potatoes on his plate with his fork. "Bubba's not really mad at anyone over the whole football field fiasco. He's just frustrated about the whole chicken wing restaurant deal. Skeeter's blaming himself, though. Between all those emotions going on, those two are both afraid that the other's mad at them, and so they're just steering clear."

None of this was news to me, of course, so I just nodded my head. "Heck, Buck, I hate it. Seeing those two not getting along is killing me. I've even tried to talk to my uncle about it, but he won't discuss it with me."

Buck set his jaw and thought for a second. "You know, I may just have a plan." He was staring off into the distance away from the building and slowly stroking his chin with his index finger and thumb. "In fact, this may be exactly what those two need."

He was quiet for a second, and I could only assume that he was working out the details in his head. Buck finally looked up, saw me staring at him, then snapped back to reality. He looked me straight in the eyes. "Huntin' trip," he said, and started nodding his head.

Now, I knew that going hunting was Buck's answer to most everything, but in this case it actually made some sense. If we got those two out in the country, they just might be able to work out any problems. "You know, Buck, you may just have a point there! How do you think we ought to go about this little endeavor?"

He looked around the patio area, then narrowed his eyes like he was imparting the top secrets of national defense to me. "Tell you what. You get your uncle over to my deer lease early Saturday morning, and I'll drag Skeeter over there for a day of turkey hunting. It'll be perfect. Thanksgiving is coming up, so we're going to need a bird, and with a little luck this will help bring everyone back together."

The more I thought about it, the better I liked the idea. "I think I can make that happen, Buck." I dug into my chopped ham and couldn't help but grin as I chewed. "That's a good idea you've got there! This ought to do the trick!" I was excited, all right. I hated seeing Uncle Bubba all torn up. It was especially bad since he was at odds with Skeeter.

We sat there and planned it all out while we ate lunch. The hunting trip had to be the way to resolve everything.

I called Uncle Bubba that night, of course, and asked him to go turkey hunting. We already had the licenses, so that wasn't a problem. As far as I knew, everyone in Cut Plug renewed their hunting and fishing license as regular as their drivers license. No one would dare be caught without one, whether they hunted or not—it'd be an incredible social blunder.

He was all for it, so I spent Friday evening cleaning my shotgun. Since I wasn't much of a hunter myself, it'd been a while since I'd been out.

I picked Uncle Bubba up that Saturday morning and started out. About ten minutes into the drive out to Buck's deer lease, he started getting curious. "Just where are you taking me hunting today, Nephew?"

I tried not to tip my hand. "Oh, we're going to go over to Buck's hunting lease. He said he might even meet us there."

All my uncle said was, "Oh." It was obvious that Uncle Bubba was still pretty bummed out from the giant armadillo incident. I knew that he saw the whole thing as another stumbling block in the way of his wing restaurant.

We arrived at the barbed-wire gate without fanfare, and my uncle hopped out to pull it open. He climbed back into the cab of my truck after closing it behind us and looked ahead at the trucks in the clearing. Both Buck's and Skeeter's vehicles were there.

Uncle Bubba's brow furrowed, and he took a deep breath. "This may not be a good idea, Nephew." He nodded at the trucks before us. "Skeeter's pretty mad at me right now."

I smiled. "Uncle Bubba, I doubt that anyone's really mad at anybody else. Let's just do some turkey hunting and see if we can't all just have a good time."

He didn't say anything. He just sat there with an apprehensive look on his face as I pulled up behind Buck's horn-adorned truck and rolled to a stop. We prepared in silence, pulling on our hunting vests and stuffing the hand-packed shotgun shells in the loops of our hunting belts. That was another thing that was common among all Cut Plug hunters—everyone loaded their own shells. Hinkley's Grocery sold the powder, wadding, and shot that any good hunter needed. Folks always saved the hulls of the shells from their last hunting trip, and in fact, most every home in Cut Plug had a paper sack full of empty hulls, just waiting to be reused.

Buck was on us before we even suspected he was there. "All right, fellows!" he said, and clapped my uncle on the back. "Glad you two could make it. We're going to get us some Thanksgiving turkeys today!" He waved his pride and joy, a Belgian-made Browning 12-gauge, out toward the fields before us.

Skeeter moseyed up and just muttered, "Hey."

Bubba nodded at him, so did Buck, and since I figured that was the appropriate thing to do, I nodded at him as well. We stood around in the early morning stillness that could only be found out in the country on a cool, early morning like this.

After my uncle and I finished loading up, the four of us headed off across the field, Buck in the lead, Uncle Bubba, Skeeter, and myself following closely behind. Occasionally someone would speak up. Buck would say, "I'll bet there's a couple of big'uns over there." I'd follow up with something like, "We're gonna eat good on Thanksgiving, then!" Uncle Bubba and Skeeter never joined in with us like we'd hoped, though.

At Buck's direction, we crossed over a couple of barbed-wire fences and any number of pastures. Conversation was sparse, and our journey was relatively quiet.

Uncle Bubba was now leading the way, followed by Skeeter and I, with Buck bringing up the rear and scouring the countryside for any sign of turkeys.

Buck must have noticed that Skeeter was being a little careless with his shotgun, because he slapped him on the shoulder and said, "Don't you know anything about hunting safety, Skeeter? Break that twelve-gauge down while you're walking."

Sure enough, Skeeter had his shotgun ready to fire, while the rest of us were walking with ours broken open over our arm, the stock and firing pin safely away from the barrel with the live ammo.

Skeeter just shook his head. "Aw, c'mon, Buck. You wouldn't believe how safe I am with this thing. Besides, you've got to pull the hammer back to fire." He made his point by doing just that. Right about then, I saw him trip, and as he was going down the still of the morning was broken with a giant *Baaaa-roooom* of a shotgun blast. About fifteen feet ahead of us, Uncle Bubba fell.

For the next few seconds, everything moved in slow motion. Skeeter leapt to his feet, screaming, and the three of us ran to Uncle Bubba. It seemed to take an eternity to reach him.

When I got there, he had rolled over onto his back, and his eyes were tightly shut. It looked like he was in an incredible amount of pain. "Uncle Bubba, are you okay?"

He opened one eye cautiously, then the other, as if he was taking stock of just how wounded he really was. At least he was alive, which allayed my greatest fear.

"Well, course I'm not okay!" he hollered. "Skeeter's gone and shot me in the butt!"

Skeeter was immediately at his side, blubbering and almost in tears. "Bubba! Bubba, I'm so sorry! I didn't mean to shoot you!" He ran his hands under my uncle, feeling the seat of the jeans. "How bad are you hurt, Bubba?"

My uncle slapped his hand away with a powerful swing. "Get your hand off my butt, Skeeter. What the heck is wrong with you, anyway. First you pretty near kill me, then you're feeling of my rear end. Ain't nobody touching my butt until we get to the hospital." He tried to sit up and grimaced. "Now you boys get me outta here right now. Hurry!"

Skeeter was beside himself with worry. "Don't fret none, Bubba, we're gonna get you to a doctor right away."

Buck turned away from Uncle Bubba, knelt down between his feet, and grabbed a leg under each arm. "Come on, you two, pick him up gently. Lift under the shoulders, and let's get him to a hospital.

The fact that Buck was even entertaining the idea of leaving the shotguns out here made me realize how seriously he was taking the situation and the danger that my uncle might really be in.

Skeeter and I carefully raised him as Buck stood up with us, and in only a moment we were trotting at a full gallop back toward the trucks. I know it wasn't a smooth ride for my uncle, because he was giving a grunt or a yell every few steps. Skeeter followed every one of them up with "I'm sorry, Bubba," or "We're going to get you some help, Bubba."

We maneuvered him through gates and over fences, until we finally reached the place we'd come in. As gently as possible, we laid him over into the bed of Buck's truck. Skeeter and I climbed in with him, positioning him in the center for as smooth a ride as possible.

Buck fired that truck up, turned it around, and sped back toward the main road.

The casualty of our hunting trip was just lying there with his eyes closed, his hands clutching mine and Skeeter's tightly. I was really worried about him, and for a second a tear welled up in my eye. "Uncle Bubba, you hang in there, now. We're going to get you to the emergency room just as fast as this pickup will fly." I saw a tear roll down Skeeter's cheek as well. My uncle just had to be all right—he just had to.

"Irma," my uncle whispered. "Get Irma."

I squeezed his hand. "I'll call her just as soon as we get you to the hospital, Uncle Bubba."

He shook his head. "No way, Nephew. You know how far the hospital is from Cut Plug. I won't have Irma driving there by herself, worrying about me every inch of the way. You tell Buck that we're going to swing by and get her."

I knew that what he was saying made sense, but I couldn't see taking the time out when he could be critically wounded. "Uncle Bubba, we're simply going to have to get you some help first."

I had more to say, but he let go of my hand and held up his index finger to silence me. "Nephew, you tell Buck to swing by the house." I could see in his eyes that there wouldn't be any give and take on the issue, so I just sighed and pounded on the back window of the truck. Buck looked around, and I yelled, "Go get Irma!"

Buck's eyes got wide, and the big man's face turned white. "You don't mean," his voice trailed off.

I shook my head and hollered back, "Naw, he just wants Aunt Irma to come along with us." Buck nodded, and steered us toward their house.

Nothing is very far from anything else in Cut Plug, so in just a matter of minutes we pulled into Uncle Bubba's driveway. Buck had started honking the horn the minute we were at the end of the block, so Aunt Irma already had her head sticking out of the front door.

"Aunt Irma, come quick!" I guess when she saw the three of us in the truck, with Skeeter and I huddled around Uncle Bubba, she knew something was wrong. My aunt crossed the yard with a speed that would have taken first place at the annual Cut Plug High School Track Meet last year.

"Bubba!" There was an ever-increasing panic in her voice. "Bubba, what happened? Are you hurt?"

She'd reached the truck by then and hopped up there with us in a flash. "Oh, Bubba!"

My uncle patted her hand. "Now don't worry, dear, I'm going to be all right. Skeeter just did a dang fool thing out there and shot me in the back end."

That, of course, launched Skeeter into another round of repentance. "Irma, I'm so terribly sorry," he wailed, "I didn't mean to shoot Bubba. I'd never, ever hurt this man. He's my best friend in the entire world!"

I decided to take the situation back under control. "Look, we're all worried about Uncle Bubba, but we'd better get him to the hospital right away!"

Aunt Irma was still surveying the damage. "Bubba, honey, roll over and let me take a look."

"I'm not about to!" He sounded like he was pretty firm on that issue. "I'll be danged if I'm going to have everyone in Cut

Plug looking at me with my butt end sticking up in the air. Let's just let the doctor take care of it."

Buck was looking back at us through the rear window, and I motioned for him to get going.

My aunt wasn't quite ready to let the issue go, though, and she held up her hand to stop him. "I'm not leaving until I see if we need to get some bandages from the house!" She was poking around on Uncle Bubba and inspecting him as best as she could without his cooperation. "Nephew, what did ya'll do to stop the bleeding?"

"Uh, nothing really." I shrugged. "There hasn't been any bleeding to stop."

Uncle Bubba sat up quickly. "Well of course there is! Skeeter blasted me in the butt with a shotgun! I probably lost it all when you three were dragging me through that field."

I guess that I'd been carried away in the crisis and had let the obvious slip by. "Uncle Bubba, if your hindquarters were full of buckshot, there's no way that it wouldn't be gushing blood. I haven't even seen a drop."

Buck had rolled his window down to hear what was going on, and he now climbed out of the cab. "Your nephew's right, Bubba." He wrinkled his brow and scratched his head. "In fact, at that close a range, I'm surprised you could even sit up and talk."

Irma crossed her arms. "Bubba, roll over!" This one was not a request.

"But, Irma," my uncle started.

"Bubba!" she barked. He looked completely defeated as he lay back down and slowly rolled over. What we saw was truly a sight to behold.

My uncle's jeans had apparently been burned away, and there were swatches missing from his white underwear. Bright pink patches of skin from his buttocks shone with an unnatural fluorescence. Aunt Irma reached down and cautiously poked at the exposed epidermis.

Bubba let out a yell that caused several of the neighbors to peek out of their windows. "Lord's sake, Irma, what are you doing back there?"

"Hmmm." Buck's eyes narrowed. "What're you shootin' with, Skeeter?"

He shrugged his shoulders. "Buckshot, just like everybody else."

Buck reached over and took a shell out of Skeeter's hunting vest. He tossed it up in the air a few times, carefully catching it and rolling it over in his hand. Next, he held it up beside his ear and shook it, starting to stare at Skeeter suspiciously. "All right, Skeeter, let's have it."

Skeeter frowned and shook his head. "I don't know what you're talking about."

Buck took out his pocketknife and used the blade to pry open the end of the red plastic shell. He then fished out way too much wadding for a normal load, then turned the shell upside down and shook out the gunpowder. "So you're not using shot, Skeeter? How long's that been going on?"

Skeeter bowed his head. "I'm sorry, you guys. I've just never been able to stand the idea of shooting an animal." His voice was cracking and his shoulders were shaking a little.

"What!" Buck yelled. I think he was genuinely shocked. "As long as you're hunting within season, and for meat, what the heck's wrong with that?"

"I don't know!" Skeeter stood up and climbed out of the truck bed, then backed away from us. "I just can't do it, that's all!"

Aunt Irma smiled. "Well I think that's just fine, Skeeter! If you hadn't been loading without the shot, my Bubba could be in pretty bad shape right now."

"What makes you think I'm not hurt the way it is?" my uncle yelled. "Now everybody stop jabberin' and get me to the hospital."

We were all quiet for a second and then Aunt Irma started laughing. Kind of soft, at first, but it grew more and more. Buck joined in, and I couldn't help but follow. Pretty soon, even Skeeter was cackling at the top of his lungs.

Uncle Bubba raised up. "I'm serious! You people get me to a doctor right this instant!"

Of course, that only made everyone laugh harder. We carried on while he lay there yelling at us. Finally, Aunt Irma shook her head. "All right, boys, help me get Bubba inside. I'll put some aloe vera on the powder burns, and he'll be just fine.

We picked him up and got him into the bedroom where Aunt Irma could work on him, and in a few minutes he came hobbling back out. He was moaning and griping all the way, but I think he was enjoying all the attention. Since he couldn't do the honors himself, he lay on the couch and shouted instructions into the kitchen for the rest of us to fix up a couple of batches of Thanksgiving chicken wings. We had to fit the recipes for the materials that Aunt Irma had in her pantry, and after a little analysis from Uncle Bubba on the couch, we had one batch of sesame chicken wings, and another of his delicious soy sauce wings. I guess that for one year, the turkeys were safe in Cut Plug.

Sesame Chicken Wings

20 chicken wings
4 cloves garlic, finely chopped
1 inch of fresh ginger, peeled and finely chopped
1 onion, quartered
1 tsp red pepper flakes
2 tsp salt
2 tsp ground coriander
3 Tbsp soy sauce
3 Tbsp fresh lemon juice
2 Tbsp sesame oil
2 Tbsp sugar
½ cup sesame seeds

Put all of the ingredients, except for the chicken wings and sesame seeds, in a blender. Set the blender to chop, and let it run for at least 30 seconds. The intent is not to liquify, but to combine all the ingredients to an even texture. Pour the mixture over the chicken and stir to coat all the pieces well. The wings need to marinate in the refrigerator for a few hours or overnight. When you're ready to begin cooking them, remove the chicken and sprinkle with the sesame seeds. Bake in preheated oven at 375 degrees for at least 45 minutes. Watch them, though, and don't let the wings burn.

Soy Sauce Wings

20 chicken wings
1 cup soy sauce
1 cup water
3 Tbsp sugar
4 Tbsp brown sugar
3 Tbsp minced garlic

2 Tbsp minced ginger
1 green onion, chopped
¼ cup cooking sherry
¼ tsp sesame oil

Mix all of the ingredients together in a pan, except for oil and wings. Bring the mixture to a boil, then lower the temperature and add the chicken wings. Let them cook for about 20-25 minutes, stirring the mixture occasionally. When the wings appear to be done, turn off the burner and allow the wings to sit for another 30 minutes, stirring them occasionally to coat evenly. Finally, add the sesame oil and crank the heat back up for a few minutes, just enough to get them ready to serve.

Spirits of Cut Plug Christmas

Christmas was a magical time, especially in Cut Plug. The town suddenly became draped in tinsel and colorful lights, and folks' entire attitude changed for the better. For a few weeks, anyway.

Describing the little town as something you'd see in a Currier and Ives snow scene was a little difficult, since we didn't get much of the frosty white powder. Sometimes it went three or four years at a stretch without a single flake falling. Still, Cut Plug at Yuletide had its own charm. A lot of the houses get caught up in trying to out-do each other with decorations, which makes for a rainbow array of color spread over the streets of town.

The Chamber of Commerce used to set up a manger scene in the town square, but Mr. Anester, the city attorney, decided one year that somebody might up and sue Cut Plug for infringing on their religious beliefs, or lack thereof. He put a stop to it immediately, so the Chamber donated the manger scene to the Cut Plug Missionary Baptist Church, where it has been every Christmas since.

Christmastime in Cut Plug was full of traditions, such as the lighting of the Holiday Tree over in front of City Hall, the Volunteer Fire Department's charity hot dog supper, and of course, the high school drama club's production of *A Christmas Carol* that they gave every year.

Some years the play was moving and touched the hearts of those in the audience, while others it was a struggle just to make it to the visit from Marley's ghost. The year that Jason Tretchor played Scrooge could have been the worst. Jason was just peaking in his march through puberty, and his voice cracked soprano with every "Bah! Humbug!"

When the night of the annual play came, I got there about the same time as Aunt Irma and Uncle Bubba, so I was able to sit beside them. All seating at the high school auditorium was first-come, first-served.

The production actually went better than I'd ever seen before. The stagehands had apparently seen one too many Steven Spielberg movies, because the play was filled with special effects, but that made it all the more interesting.

The knocker on Scrooge's door came to life, the bell in his bedroom rang mysteriously by itself, and Marley literally flew onto the stage. You could hardly see the rope that they'd painted black to suspend him from.

All in all, it was the best Christmas play we'd had as far back as I could remember. My uncle sat there in rapt attention, seemingly fascinated by the whole affair. That's why it surprised me so much when I got back to my seat after intermission and Uncle Bubba wasn't there. I leaned over to ask Aunt Irma what had happened to him, and she just whispered back, "Bubba said there was something he had to take care of, so he took off with Skeeter and Buck. Said they had some important lodge business."

I figured that Uncle Bubba had just gotten bored with the play, so I didn't give his absence a second thought. That is, until about one o'clock in the morning when Aunt Irma woke me up with a phone call.

"Nephew, do you have any idea what kind of lodge business Bubba could be on?" She didn't sound sleepy; she sounded worried. "He still isn't home."

Of course, I didn't know about anything in particular going on with the Armadillos that night. "Oh, who knows, with all the secret committees and everything the fellows have. I wouldn't worry a bit, Aunt Irma. I'm sure he's just fine." I really believed that he was, but I knew my aunt was worried about him. "Tell you what. I'll hop in my truck and see if I can't find him for you."

"Aw, I hate to get you out of bed in the middle of the night like that." There was a hesitation in her voice, though, which told me it would help her feelings immensely if I did that very thing.

"Aunt Irma, it won't be a bit of trouble. I'll find him, send him home, and be back in bed in fifteen minutes. You just try to go to sleep—I'll have Uncle Bubba back in no time at all!" I gave her a few more words of reassurance, then pulled on a pair of white shorts that I kept by the bed. It was cold outside, but quite honestly, I didn't plan on leaving the heated comfort of my truck's cab.

In only a minute, I was tooling down the dark country road that led to Junior Newton's barn. After all, that was the official Armadillo meeting hall. As I got closer I didn't see any lights on inside, and my headlights quickly revealed that there wasn't anyone else around.

I rolled down my window and leaned my head outside— there wasn't a sound to be heard. My nose picked up the faint whiff of charcoal in the air, though, which led me to a single inevitable conclusion: Uncle Bubba had been here and had more than likely been grilling up some wings. The cold was starting to nip away at me, so I quickly rolled up the window and tried to figure where to look next. It was becoming more apparent that I should have gotten dressed before starting on this excursion. Nevertheless, I turned the truck around and headed back.

Cut Plug was small enough that the entire town could be covered in short order, so I decided to start at the town square and work my way out.

When I was only a few blocks away, I hit pay dirt. Parked on the side of the street was my Uncle's truck, then Skeeter's, and finally Buck's, with the majestic deer horns perched proudly on front.

The guys were nowhere to be seen, though. The streetlights gave enough illumination for me to make that determination. I wondered if they could be visiting someone on the block, but it would have been very uncharacteristic of Uncle Bubba not to tell Aunt Irma where he was.

Still, I didn't see any signs of activity. I figured I'd make a quick pass through the next block or so, then I could legitimately go home, call Aunt Irma, and tell her that Bubba and the fellows were just over at someone's house.

I was satisfied with the plan, and after driving around for a minute more, had actually started accelerating toward home. That's when I passed Mr. Trickle's house.

I caught something out of the corner of my eye. It was unusual enough that I quickly threw on the brakes, then backed around so that my headlights swept the front yard. Standing there were three figures. The first was a skinny fellow wrapped in what could only be aluminum foil. The second was a muscular man in a green bathrobe, red boots, and a huge bundle of holly wrapped around the top of his head. The third, and most ominous, was a figure in a black robe that appeared to be a sheet wrapped clumsily around his ample torso and up over his head.

I quickly parked the truck and jumped out of the cab. "Uncle Bubba, just what in the wide world are you fellows doing out here?"

Uncle Bubba looked at me like he was in shock that I'd dare to interrupt whatever scheme they were acting out. "Nephew!" he called out, his voice quieted. "Get over here!"

It only took a few moments for me to cross the yard, but in my bare feet, the last few steps were torture on the cold grass. "I'm serious! What are the three of you doing out here?" Up close, their costumes were even more bizarre than I'd first thought. Skeeter was wrapped in foil head to toe, with the sheets held precariously together with duct tape. I was hoping that he was wearing something underneath, because it was obvious that one wrong move would easily split the foil, and I certainly didn't want to be around for that. All in all, he appeared to be ready for some futuristic remake of *The Mummy*.

Buck looked even more ridiculous. The green garment was obviously a woman's fluffy bathrobe, and it was even trimmed in little white flowers. He had on red cowboy boots, the Little Red Riders that most ladies owned, and it was pretty clear that they were a good size or two under what his feet actually needed. Lord only knows who they really belonged to. The holly on his head was actually a wreath, and I thought it looked suspiciously like the one from the front door of my uncle's house. If that was the case, and Aunt Irma found out, there'd be hell to pay over it. Since the wreath was so leafy, the hole in the middle wasn't quite large enough for Buck's head to poke through. It was perched on top like some kind of holly-covered sombrero.

Uncle Bubba's costume wasn't the black shroud that I had originally imagined when I first pulled up. It was, in fact, Aunt Irma's dark blue bed sheet that she used when company came to visit. It was pulled tight around his belly, and thrown up over his head so that only his face was peeking out.

My uncle held his finger to his lips to quiet me. "Shhhh! You're going to spoil everything, Nephew. And what are you doing out here half nekkid in the cold?"

The meager pair of shorts I had donned were feeling more and more thin as the icy air dug into me. I really hadn't planned on stepping outside of my truck. As I studied the trio in front of me, though, I didn't feel so underdressed. "Just what are these getups?" I whispered. "Why are the three of you dressed up in some kind of bad Halloween gear?"

Uncle Bubba gave me an ear-to-ear grin like he was right on top of the situation. "This plan is the one that's going to do it for me. It's finally going to get the old tightwad to lend me some money for the wing restaurant." He rared back proudly. "You see, Skeeter here's the Ghost of Christmas Past, Buck is the Ghost of Christmas Present, and I'm the Ghost of Christmas Yet to Come—just like in the play by that Dickens fellow! Nephew, we're fixing to haunt banker Trickle!"

I was speechless for a moment. I honestly had no idea what to say to my uncle. I knew, however, that I somehow had to drag this madness to a screeching halt. "Uncle Bubba, what could have possibly made you think this infernal scheme would work? This is hands down, no contest, the worst idea you've ever had. And as much as I hate to say it, you've had some pretty bad ones in your time!"

My uncle started waving his hand at me. "No, no, no, Nephew, you don't understand! Trickle's going to think he's dreaming, as each of us go in there and whisper stuff in his ear about what a Scrooge he is, how much better he'd feel if he gave me the loan, and little gems of wisdom like that. If he were to open his eyes, he'd only see our ghostly forms. That'd convince him it was a dream for sure."

I couldn't believe what I was hearing. All I could do was stand there, shaking my head. "Uncle Bubba, you must be crazy. You boys haven't been drinking, have you?"

"Why, of course not!" Uncle Bubba seemed wounded that I would question their actions. Skeeter and Buck stood beside him looking innocent. "All we did was cook some habanero honey wings at Junior's barn while we waited for the right time to launch my plan."

"That's right," Skeeter spoke up. "Bubba grilled while we got the costumes ready."

"I'm not believing that the three of you thought those costumes would work. If I'd been five minutes later, it would be Deputy Hernandez standing in front of me, and I'd be trying to talk him into letting you all go." I was getting more and more frustrated. It was insane. "We're talking about breaking and entering, for crying out loud!"

"Oh, now, Nephew, there you go again." I could see that any logic I was offering was still being lost on my uncle. "You're trying to make something bad out of a simple idea. You know that no one locks their doors in Cut Plug. We wouldn't be breaking in anywhere."

"But, Uncle Bubba," I pleaded. "In the eyes of the law, once you crossed through that door, you'd be a criminal!"

The three of them looked shocked, like they'd never even considered that option before. "You think?" Uncle Bubba asked.

I simply nodded my head. Right about then is when the porch light snapped on, and we were all bathed in a brilliant white light.

We were all in shock for a second, and I searched for any cover story. The front door opened, and in desperation, I started to sing: "God rest ye merry gentlemen, let nothing you dismay!" I shot the trio behind me as stern a glare as I could muster, then kept on going.

The fellows slowly joined in, combining their voices with mine, "Remember Christ our Savior was born on Christmas Day!"

Mr. Trickle threw the door open and practically leapt out onto the porch. "What the hell's going on out there? Bubba, is that you in that sheet?" He turned back toward the house. "I'm calling the law, that's what I'm going to do!"

I had to think fast. "Uh, Mr. Trickle, I thought you knew about the church's midnight caroling program. Didn't you sign up to be sung to tonight?" I tried to sound as genuine as I could. Believe me, it was tough, knowing that those three were huddled behind me in those foolish costumes.

Trickle turned around and eyed me suspiciously. "I don't have a clue what you're talking about. Besides, how come the four of you are dressed up like idiots? You don't look like carolers to me."

"Oh, sure we are!" I turned around and gestured at the spirits. "Can't you tell that these are the Ghosts of Christmas Past, Present, and Future?"

He looked around me to study Bubba and the boys. "Well," Trickle said slowly, "maybe so. But who are you supposed to be, standing out here in your underwear? You're indecently exposed out here on my front lawn!"

I just stood there, my mind blank. I had no clue how to weave myself into this impromptu pageant.

Finally, I heard Skeeter chime in, "Don't you know anything, Trickle? He's Baby New Year!"

I could feel my entire body turning crimson with embarrassment. I was going to throttle Skeeter when I got ahold of him later. Mr. Trickle glared at me for a few moments, then just grunted. "Well, just move on. I don't want you singing out in front of my house, church program or not." He stormed inside and slammed the door.

We stood there silently, until Buck finally said, "If there's any man in Cut Plug that needs haunting by the Christmas ghosts, it's that fella there."

I just shook my head and started walking back to my truck. Uncle Bubba and the other guys were heading for theirs as well. "Hey, Nephew!" my uncle called. "We still have a few wings back at Junior's barn. Want to meet us there to finish them up?"

It didn't sound like a bad offer at all. "Tell you what, Uncle Bubba. You swing by and tell Aunt Irma where you're going, and I'm going to stop at my house and pick up some clothes. I'll meet you all at the Armadillo lodge in a quarter-hour."

I drove away, marveling at how Uncle Bubba had dodged yet another bullet. That man led a charmed life. He was also a fantastic cook, and I was looking forward to a middle-of-the-night snack of the habanero honey wings. As I drove away, I couldn't help but sing under my breath, "God rest ye merry gentlemen, let nothing you dismay. . ."

Habanero Honey Wings

20 chicken wings
2 eggs
¼ cup melted butter or margarine
¼ cup soy sauce
¼ cup lemon juice
¾ cup honey
2 Tbsp habanero sauce
2 Tbsp minced garlic
2 habanero peppers, sliced thinly

Beat the two eggs in a bowl, then add all other ingredients except the wings. Make sure you mix everything well.

Next, coat each wing in the sauce and place them on a greased cookie sheet. Aunt Irma always insisted on using a vegetable spray, just to make it a healthier recipe. Bake for approximately 45 minutes or until the chicken is thoroughly cooked. Basting the wings a couple of times during the process makes them taste that much better!

25

The Valentine's Beauty Pageant Ultimatum

*U*ncle Bubba passed through the holiday season without further incident, and the new year was on us before we all knew it.

As the days went by, I knew that Uncle Bubba had been getting more and more down over the lack of progress on his chicken wing restaurant. That's why I was so excited when I discovered what I considered to be the perfect opportunity for Uncle Bubba to promote himself as a chicken wing aficionado. It was February, which meant that the annual Cut Plug Sweetheart Pageant was at hand.

I knew the preparation for the Valentine's Day event was always catered, usually by one of the local organizations. The Book of Ruth Bible class did it three years ago, then the Volunteer Firefighters Wives' Auxiliary, and last year the Cut Plug Garden Club provided the spread.

The food was actually served a few hours before the pageant, since all the folks who were a part of it were at the high school auditorium all day getting ready. The Volunteer Fire Department band was getting set up, the girls were rehearsing their group songs and dances, and the decorating committee was busy beautifying the auditorium to make it look a little less Cut Plug and a little more Atlantic City.

It apparently helped out if a buffet was served over the course of the afternoon, so people could come up and nibble as they pleased without taking too much time away from their duties.

I figured this would be the perfect opportunity for Uncle Bubba to get a mention in the program as a catering service, which would almost be as good has having the restaurant open. It would be a first step, anyway.

When I saw him at the cement plant the next day, I brought up the idea to him. He cocked his head to one side and thought about it for a minute. Finally, a smile crossed his face. "Nephew, I think you may have hit on a dandy there." He was staring off into space for a minute, then begin nodding his head. "I'll bet that once word gets around about my wings, banker Trickle will be begging me to take a loan from him to open the restaurant!"

While I really didn't share his optimism to that degree, I thought it would at least be good exposure. I left Uncle Bubba standing there, mulling over the whole situation.

The very next day, he came running up to me in the plant's cafeteria. "Nephew!" he yelled from the other side of the room. "Nephew, I did it!" He snaked his way through the luncheon crowd over to my table.

"I talked to Mrs. Tetwiler last night, and not only am I going to be the official caterer for this year's pageant, but I'm going to be a judge!" He stood there with his shoulders thrown back, obviously proud of his accomplishment.

I gave him a hearty congratulation, with only a little reserve. While I genuinely felt like this was going to be a step in the right direction for him, I sincerely doubted that it would make any immediate changes at all in Mr. Trickle's resolve like Uncle Bubba was hoping for.

The hoopla surrounding the pageant grew exponentially as each day passed. Rumors were flying about who was going to be wearing what type of dress, and the seamstresses of the town were holed up in their sewing rooms making plans with more secrecy than our boys used back at the D-Day invasion.

When the big day finally arrived, Uncle Bubba recruited me to help with the catering. We went over that afternoon and set up a long table in front of the stage so that it would be out of the way but would still be accessible to all the pageant participants. The hustle and bustle around us was incredible. With the way everyone was carrying on, you would have thought the Miss Universe Pageant had been moved to Cut Plug by some horrible mistake. Every contestant was rehearsing, fretting, or crying with at least a mother in tow, and sometimes an aunt or grand-mother as well.

The boys in the Volunteer Fire Department band were doing their best to run through the music, and God love 'em, their hearts were in the right place. There were five members: a drummer, a bass guitarist, a trumpeter, a saxophonist, and the fire chief himself, Big Ed Ernest, on keyboards. Fortunately for Cut Plug, they were better firefighters than musicians.

When Uncle Bubba and I had everything set up, he finally peeled back the foil from the top of the pans holding the wings and the place fell silent. The aroma of those beauties filled the auditorium, and everyone's nose pointed toward the ceiling in a unison sniff.

He'd made four different varieties just so that everyone could find something they liked: marinated herb wings, apricot wings, red wine wings, and even sweet and sour chicken wings. On the way to the auditorium, we'd stopped by the grocery store to pick up a few tubs of Mrs. Hinkley's mustard potato salad, and Aunt Irma had sent a big crock pot full of baked beans. The lines formed quickly, and the pageant personnel did some serious damage to the buffet in only a matter of minutes.

Uncle Bubba stood behind the table, proudly accepting the accolades and congratulations for such a job well done. I have to admit, they were well deserved. My uncle had outdone himself this time.

In just a little over an hour the pans were all empty, so we folded the table back up and took everything out to the truck. When we got there, a white envelope was tucked under the driver's side windshield wiper blade. Uncle Bubba pulled it out and opened it, and as he read the paper inside I saw an odd look cross his face.

"You okay, Uncle Bubba?" I didn't have a clue what it was, but it was certainly something that had rattled him.

He just nodded his head. We finished loading the truck in silence. Whatever was in that note certainly had him preoccupied.

That evening I rode to the pageant with him and Aunt Irma, and since I had helped with the catering, I got to sit beside my aunt on the first row. The judges' table was right in front of us, and there were three of them this year. Deputy Hernandez was sitting in the middle between banker Trickle and Uncle Bubba. Aunt Irma had already stood up twice to go brush something off his jacket. I think she was just proud that she'd managed to get him into a suit.

I could see there was still something bothering my uncle, but I couldn't figure out what. He kept glancing around nervously. Once I saw him lock gazes with the banker, and Uncle Bubba looked quickly down at the floor. Mr. Trickle just stared at him coldly. Something was definitely wrong.

The lights suddenly came down, and the Volunteer Fire Department band struck up a lively tune. The curtains parted, and fifteen of Cut Plug's beauties began their big opening number. Mr. Underwood had brought his microphone system from the hardware store and was therefore the emcee for the evening. He stood over at one side of the stage smiling.

I wasn't watching the pageant, though. I was studying Uncle Bubba. He was sweating and fidgeting and certainly didn't seem to have his heart in the role of judge. He was hardly taking any notes.

The girls made it through the bathing suit competition, and the talent competition seemed to drag on all night. Most of the girls were in the high school band, so the majority of the competition was split between musical solos and baton twirling. Francie Engle had decided to twirl flaming batons, and predictably enough, it didn't take her two minutes to catch the curtains on fire. Another good reason for having the Cut Plug Volunteer Fire Department in attendance, I supposed. Once the blaze caught up, the fellows dropped their instruments and went to work. They grabbed fire extinguishers from back stage and had everything under control in no time at all. They sprayed the curtains down and squirted Francie down since she was still holding the batons. Mr. Underwood announced a brief intermission to get the stage cleaned up.

Uncle Bubba heaved a very disturbed sigh, then stood up. He made a fist, tucked his little finger behind his ear, and waggled his thumb behind his head. He turned and strode down the aisle of the auditorium. It was the sign of the Armadillo. I didn't know who it was for, but if something was wrong with my uncle, I was going to be there.

I jumped up and followed him outside. Skeeter and Buck weren't far behind me. They obviously saw the sign as well.

Uncle Bubba was standing out in the parking lot leaning up against his truck. I don't know when I've ever seen him look so low. His head was bowed down, his hands were in his pockets, and he was just staring down at the gravel.

I leaned up against the pickup truck beside him. "Looks like you've got something weighing pretty heavy on you, Uncle."

He reached inside his jacket pocket and handed me an envelope. Skeeter and Buck had joined us, and they crowded around while I opened it. Inside, there was a single piece of paper with a handwritten note: *Bubba, if you know what's good for you, you'll stop by the bank this afternoon—Trickle.*

"That's from banker Trickle?" Skeeter asked.

Buck reached over and popped him on the arm. "Well of course it is!" He took the paper out of my hand. "What's all this about, Bubba?"

Uncle Bubba took a long, slow breath. "That was on my windshield this afternoon. I did like he asked and dropped in after we cleaned up the wings today." He shrugged his shoulders. "I guess I got the best possible news that I could. And the worst."

"What in the world are you talking about?" Skeeter's brow wrinkled. "What kind of news?"

My uncle looked up with a frown. "He showed me a signed loan application form. Said that all I needed to do was fill it out, and I could finally get my restaurant open."

"Why, Bubba, that's great!" Skeeter said and clapped him on the back. "That's what you've been wanting!"

I could see that Uncle Bubba wasn't happy about it, though. There had to be more to the story.

"Yep." He was moving the toe of his boot around in the gravel, and he kicked one of the larger pebbles across the parking lot. "'Cept that he wants me to do him a favor. The biggest depositor at the bank's daughter is in the pageant, and he wants me to vote for her. He will too, which will make sure that little Rita Hinkley wins the whole thing."

Buck guffawed. "That homely girl?"

While it was true that Rita wasn't the most beautiful flower in the garden, she had the reputation of being an "A" student and a good kid. "C'mon now, Buck, it's not that girl's fault. What I can't figure out is why Trickle'd stick his neck out for something like that."

"Aw, shoot. That's the easy part." Uncle Bubba shook his head. "He's afraid that Hinkley might up and move his account to one of the banks in the big city since they're offering better interest rates." He stood up and paced the length of the truck. "So, all it takes to get my restaurant is to vote for that girl to win the pageant. But there's more."

I was afraid that I'd already guessed the other side to this coin. "I suppose he laid down some consequences if you don't vote his way, right, Uncle?"

He nodded. "Yep. If I don't vote for that girl, he told me that he'd make sure I never got the money to open the restaurant." Uncle Bubba paused for a second. "He said that he'd make it his life's work to stop me from ever having it."

There were a few moments of silence in the night as we all weighed the gravity of Trickle's words. I think we were all afraid to advise Uncle Bubba one way or the other. We didn't want him to do the banker's terrible bidding, but on the other hand, we all knew how much that restaurant meant to him.

Bubba must have realized that the break was about over, because he stopped for a second, looked at us, then turned and stalked off toward the auditorium. It was then that I heard my uncle utter the deepest curse that had probably ever passed his lips. "God damn that man," my uncle said softly. "God damn him to hell, playing with people's lives like that."

He stomped all the way down to the judges' table and plopped into the chair. I took my place beside Aunt Irma and wondered just what my uncle was going to do. I was nervous for him, and while I was sitting there waiting for the pageant to get started again, I wished for a helping of the wings that we'd served earlier. As I remembered them, I figured there were at least a few good things in this terrible day.

Sweet and Sour Wings

20 chicken wings
1 cup cornstarch
2 eggs
¾ cup sugar
½ cup chicken broth
4 Tbsp catsup
4 Tbsp soy sauce
1 tsp minced garlic
¼ cup vinegar

Mix all ingredients together except for chicken wings, cornstarch, and eggs. Bring to a boil, then turn down the heat and simmer while you're preparing the wings.

Wash the chicken wings, then roll them in cornstarch. Beat the eggs in a bowl, and coat each wing with egg. Dip the chicken wings in the sauce mixture, then bake them on a greased cookie sheet at 325 degrees for 45 minutes to an hour. Bring the sauce to a boil again, remove the wings from the oven, and baste one more time. Let the wings stand a few minutes before serving.

Red Wine Chicken Wings

20 chicken wings
1 cup red wine
⅓ cup soy sauce
⅓ cup orange juice
2 cloves garlic
2 Tbsp ginger root
6 Tbsp red currant jelly

Chop the ginger root and garlic cloves finely. Next, combine soy sauce, orange juice, wine, jelly, garlic, and ginger together in a large bowl. Add the wings, cover the bowl, and marinate overnight.

When you're ready to prepare them, preheat your oven to 375 degrees. Bake the wings on a cookie sheet or shallow pan that has been sprayed with vegetable spray. After 20 minutes, remove them and brush with marinade. Bake another 25 minutes or until done.

Apricot Chicken Wings

20 chicken wings
½ cup all purpose flour
½ tsp salt
1 tsp cardamom
½ cup apricot preserves
1 Tbsp Dijon mustard
½ cup nonfat yogurt

Preheat oven to 375 degrees. Wet the chicken wings and then pat them slightly to get rid of the excess water. Mix the flour, salt, and cardamom in a bowl and coat each wing thoroughly.

Bake the wings 20 minutes. While they're cooking combine the preserves, mustard, and yogurt. Remove wings from the oven and spread the apricot mixture over them. Cover with foil and bake for another 20-25 minutes.

Marinated Herb Chicken Wings

20 chicken wings
1 cup white wine
3 Tbsp olive oil
2 tsp basil
2 tsp oregano
½ tsp minced onion
3 cloves garlic, minced

Combine the wine, oil, onion, garlic, and spices together in bowl, then add the chicken wings and marinate in the refrigerator overnight. Make sure the wings are completely coated.

These wings can be done on the grill or in the oven. To bake, use a 375-degree oven and cook for about 45 minutes. If you're grilling, wait until the coals just start to gray, then put the wings on. In either case, turn and baste periodically while they cook.

Wings of Love

ittle Rita didn't win that night. My uncle voted with his heart, uninfluenced by Trickle's threats. Trickle's gaze might as well have contained daggers when Mr. Underwood read the results into the microphone.

When it was all over, my uncle was out of there in a heartbeat. The look on his face defied description. It was the hollow gaze of a beaten man. I was finally able to catch up with him in the parking lot. "You okay, Uncle Bubba?" I asked.

He was unlocking the door of his truck. "Sure." He opened the door and climbed inside, and I could see that his eyes were glistening. "You know, the cement plant isn't such a bad place to work. Hell, another ten years and I'll retire." Uncle Bubba looked away from me, then hung his head.

At that particular moment, the oddest thing occurred. Aunt Irma passed by and grabbed me by my arm. She practically dragged me to the back of the pickup. In only an instant, she had spoken a few words that would live in my memory forever, even though I didn't understand them at the time.

Aunt Irma then announced to Uncle Bubba and I that she was riding home with some of her lady friends, so I climbed in the cab of the truck with my uncle. "You know, Uncle, there's something I have to do. Mind running an errand with me?"

He sighed heavily and rested his head back against the rear window. "Nephew, I'd do most anything for you, but tonight I'd really just prefer to go home."

"Oh, come on, Uncle Bubba. This'll just take a second." I was using my most hopeful tone.

He shook his head, and put the truck in gear. "Okay, Nephew, okay. Tell me where you need to go and I'll get you there."

"Great!" I slapped my leg for emphasis. "Head for the county line, then. I need to make a beer run."

Uncle Bubba looked over at me and seemed annoyed by my request. "Nephew, I've probably got a six-pack out in my garage icebox, so why don't I just lend that to you. It'd save us from having to go all the way out there and back tonight."

"I appreciate the offer, but I need a little more than that." I was improvising. I couldn't let him resolve things that quickly. "I really need to stock up for a party I'm having for the folks in my crew at work tomorrow night."

Uncle Bubba looked over at me, and I saw the most pathetic eyes I've ever seen. "You don't mean to tell me that you're having a party and I'm not invited, do you?"

This was really killing me, and even though I didn't know what Aunt Irma had in mind, I had to keep up my end of the illusion that she'd asked for. "Well, Uncle Bubba, this is just a get-together for my crew. You know full well I'd invite you to any bona-fide party I was throwing. Hey—I'd even hire your wing catering service to handle the food!"

He frowned but pulled out of the parking lot. The ride out there was deathly quiet. Neither one of us said a word.

I knew that Uncle Bubba wasn't mad at me, however, or even annoyed about running me on the errand. He was just frustrated with the evening's events. I hated to dwell on it, but that was one defeated man in the pickup truck with me. It was terrible, watching him sink lower and lower.

He didn't even get out of the truck when we got to the package store at the county line. I went inside, got a case of good Texas beer, and plopped it down in the bed of the truck. When I climbed back in the cab, I tried to give my uncle a little encouragement. "You know, Uncle Bubba, there are probably a hundred ways to finance this thing without banker Trickle. We'll just have to keep working on it."

He didn't say anything for a long time, and we were a good third of the way back to Cut Plug when he finally shook his head slowly from side to side. "Nope. Afraid not, Nephew. I've spent a year trying to come up with something, and if there really was a way, I'd have hit on it by now." There was another pause as he drove through the night, staring straight ahead at the road. "Besides," he finally added, "it's more than that now. The stakes were a lot higher tonight. When Trickle said that he'd keep me from ever opening a restaurant, he meant it. That no-good fellow sits on every ruling body in town, from the zoning committee to the Chamber of Commerce. He'll be good to his word. You can bet your life on that."

He got quiet again, and I decided it was probably best to leave him alone for a while. We were just outside of the Cut Plug city limits, when I snapped my fingers. "Oh, no, Uncle Bubba! I went off and left my wallet back at the package store. We've got to go back and get it!"

My uncle closed his eyes and sighed. "Nephew, please. Let me just take you to your truck, and you can make the run back out there. I'm just too tired."

"But Uncle Bubba, I've got everything in there," I pleaded. "My ID, my credit cards, and even the money from the paycheck that I cashed last week. I'd hate to think it was going to be sitting on the counter for that long."

He shook his head. "Don't worry, the fellow that runs the place has probably already found it and put it safely away in the cash drawer for you. Another few minutes won't hurt."

"Look, Uncle Bubba, you've just got to help me out." I wasn't an actor, but I was doing my dead-level best to convince him. "We have to turn around and go get my wallet!"

I could tell that he wasn't happy, but he turned the truck around and we made the trip once again. He was looking worse by the mile, and I felt guilty about heaping the additional misery on him. Still, I was following Aunt Irma's orders the best I could.

We arrived at the package store, where I went in and bought a package of gum. I'd had my wallet with me all along, of course.

The trip back took forever, and not a single word was spoken. It was an especially dark evening, I noticed. Out in the country, like we were in Cut Plug, you could generally see the moon casting a silver pallor on the Texas countryside. Tonight, though, there was only a pitch-black night with our headlights cutting through it.

We were tooling down the main road that ran through town. Generally speaking, after about eight o'clock the city pretty much folded up, and you could only tell that you were passing through by the few streetlights on the main road.

Tonight, though, something bright caught my eye in the distance ahead of us. I certainly hadn't seen it on the way out. But we'd already passed the school, so whatever it was would have been behind us as we left Cut Plug.

Uncle Bubba wrinkled his brow. "What'd you suppose that light is, Nephew?"

"I don't know, Uncle." And I really didn't. "Maybe your flying saucer's come back and landed and the aliens are out looking for Skeeter."

My uncle shot a hard glance over to me. "Nephew, you do believe that UFO was real, don't you?"

"Uncle Bubba, what I believe is that we ought to check this out. It looks like something's going on up there, which is more than a little out of line for this time of night in Cut Plug."

As we got closer, the source of all the light became obvious. "Why, that's Sanderson's old filling station." Uncle Bubba vocalized what we were both thinking.

Sure enough, the place was lit up like it was still open—which it hadn't been for over a year now. When old man Sanderson passed on, his widow had just let the gas station sit.

Bubba began to slow the truck down as we approached. "Nephew, what in the world do you suppose is going on?" He leaned forward, studying the building for clues.

It was surrounded by pickups and cars, and I could see that there were quite a few people walking around inside. The huge garage doors were pulled down, but since they were windowed, a lot of activity was visible through the panes. My uncle stood on the brakes, stopping the truck. He stared at the building for a minute and finally said, "What the heck is all this about?"

I just shook my head in wonder. "Pull in, and let's check it out for ourselves." I was starting to have my suspicions, of course. After the pageant, Aunt Irma had whispered in my ear, "It's time for me to help my Bubba. Get him out of town for a while. Give me an hour, then bring him back."

Well, I'd done my part, and by that point, I was as curious as Uncle Bubba probably was. He parked the truck, and we climbed out. The more I inspected the filling station, the more changes I saw.

The old repair bays were gone, and there were tables inside with red checkered tablecloths and a candle burning in a jar on the middle of each one. Instead of the grungy walls of the garage that I remembered for all those years, I could see that a new coat of beige paint had been added.

Uncle Bubba stopped walking. "Do you have any idea what's going on here, Nephew?" There was a tone to his voice that I didn't recognize. He sounded half-hopeful, half scared to death.

People were scurrying around inside, and I couldn't help but laugh. I couldn't say for sure what was going on, but I was starting to have some extremely strong suspicions. "Come on, Uncle. Let's go inside and find out what all this is about."

I followed him to the door. It was a heavy, red number—the kind they made a few decades ago, not the glass and chrome jobs that are everywhere today. My uncle looked back at me one more time. All I could do was shrug my shoulders and smile. He turned the rusty knob and pulled the door open. We were suddenly bathed in bright light and music. Uncle Bubba took one step inside, then stopped there, silent.

The next few seconds seemed to take forever to pass, as I soaked in the whole scene. The inside of the old filling station had been magically transformed into a small, intimate restaurant. The repair bays were now the dining room. The floors were still concrete, but they were spotless. The front counter area of the station had been changed into a small reception foyer with a wooden bench and a couple of rocking chairs. Finally, and probably the crowning touch, was the storage area that was right behind the bays. A hole had been knocked in the wall separating it from the dining room, and I could see two old industrial stoves back there, which were probably the source of the wonderful aromas that were wafting through the air. Someone had gone to a lot of trouble to frame out the window perfectly, so that the entire kitchen was visible. And there were people everywhere, all smiling at us.

The Cut Plug Volunteer Fire Department band had apparently torn down their set at the beauty pageant and set back up in the corner of the filling station, and they were playing a rousing rendition of "Hot Time in the Old Town Tonight."

I looked over at Uncle Bubba, and he was still standing there like a statue. Right about then, Aunt Irma came running from the kitchen, her arms outstretched and a huge grin on her face. "Bubba!" she yelled, and hit him like a cement truck from the plant.

My aunt hugged that man so tight I thought he might squirt out of her arms, then she finally pulled back. "Bubba, I was getting tired of all your schemes to get enough money to open your wing restaurant, so I figured I was either going to go crazy, or just have to do something about it myself."

"But, Irma," he stammered. "How?"

"Oh, I still have a few tricks up my sleeve." Aunt Irma looked over and winked at me. "Where'd you think all that money I made from selling my biscotti was going, Bubba?"

I could see that my uncle's eyes were moist, and Aunt Irma reached up, brushed some of the tears away, and gave him a kiss. "I saved all that money, plus a few things here and there, like the prize you won from racing my car that night, and made a down payment on the service station." She stopped and looked around the room. "I had a little help, of course. The ladies in my Sunday school class did the tablecloths and curtains."

I saw the ladies from the Book of Ruth Bible class, still in their dress clothes from the beauty pageant, all peeking through the window from the kitchen.

Aunt Irma continued on. "And I enlisted a few of your friends to get the place fixed up over the last couple of weeks. I was gonna wait until everything was finished, but you looked like you really needed it tonight." She paused for a second. "Besides, it's Valentine's Day. What better present could I possibly give you?"

Everyone around the room was getting misty-eyed: people from the church, from Uncle Bubba's crew at the plant, and even a few youngsters from the pageant. I saw Deputy Hernandez standing over by Mr. Abernathy, hopefully not getting any tax advice, and Little Ernie Fratwhiler was taking up a full corner of the dining room just by himself.

Aunt Irma took my uncle's hand. "But all I really did was to get the ball rolling—it'll be up to you to make this thing enough of a success to keep making the payments." She hugged him again, then stood up and squared her shoulders. "Now come on, let me show you around your new restaurant!" She led him toward the kitchen, my uncle following in some kind of blissful state.

As Uncle Bubba and Aunt Irma disappeared, Skeeter, Effie, and Buck walked up. I narrowed my eyes at them. "So, did you folks know about this and just keep it from me?"

They all laughed, and Effie Marie shook her head. "Nope. We all found out an hour ago, right after you disappeared with Bubba after the beauty pageant. Apparently, Irma was afraid one of us might let it slip." She turned and put her arm around Skeeter. "The band's been playing too long for me to go without a dance. Let's push some of the tables out of the way so you can show me your moves!" Effie strode away with Skeeter in tow.

Buck leaned over to me and in a whisper asked, "Does Skeeter actually know how to dance?"

I shrugged my shoulders. "You know, Buck, I've never even seen him try. He just might surprise us all." I thought about it for a second, then had to ask the question that was foremost on my mind. "So if Aunt Irma has everything set up, do you think Uncle Bubba can make a go of this place?"

Buck thought about it for a moment, then nodded his head. "Yep, I think he can. That is, if anyone can make a business run in Cut Plug."

I had to agree. Uncle Bubba would figure out some way to pull this thing off.

Everything came to a screeching halt as the ladies from the Book of Ruth Bible class paraded out of the kitchen carrying trays of chicken wings, which the crowd immediately flocked around. Pastor Frawley stepped up to give the blessing of the food and then everyone dug in.

I later found out that Aunt Irma had asked for volunteers to make their favorite wing recipes for the big celebration, and I have to say that the people of Cut Plug who were in attendance outdid themselves.

I assumed that Uncle Bubba was inspecting every inch of his restaurant, because I hadn't seen him for quite a while, but I made sure to try at least one of every type of wing there that night. I also made a point to track down the chefs and record their recipes, just so Uncle Bubba would have them.

It was a grand evening, to say the least. I don't know when I've ever seen my Uncle Bubba happier, and the sparkle in his eye was probably the perfect reward for Aunt Irma.

Notes From the Cab of the Pickup

All the wings were delicious that night, and I know for a fact that Uncle Bubba used many of them on the first pass of his menu. Of course, he was continually changing it up for variety in the months that followed, but the recipes that night were a fantastic start. It was in the wee hours of the next morning when I left Uncle Bubba's new wing restaurant, and the last thing I saw was my aunt and uncle doing a slow two-step to a romantic number being played by the Cut Plug Volunteer Fire Department band.

Now that Uncle Bubba had his restaurant, I wondered if it would be the end to all of his planning, scheming, and mischief.

In the solitude of my pickup, I fired the engine and just had to laugh. Of course it wouldn't. As with all things in Uncle Bubba's life, it was just the beginning of another story.

Deputy Hernandez' Hot Honey Barbecue Wings

20 chicken wings
1 cup of your favorite barbecue sauce
½ cup honey
2 Tbsp lemon juice
1 tsp cayenne pepper

This is a simple recipe. It also allows you to tweak the flavor by using your favorite barbecue sauce. It can be an off-the-shelf variety from the grocery store or your favorite family recipe.

Combine the barbecue sauce, honey, lemon juice, and cayenne pepper together in a bowl. Marinate the wings in the mixture overnight, and save the sauce when you start cooking them.

This recipe is equally tasty on the grill or in the oven, so take your pick. The oven should be preheated at 375 degrees or the coals in your grill allowed to gray before starting.

Cook the wings for 10 minutes, then baste with the marinade. Repeat this every 10 minutes until the wings are done, approximately 45 minutes. After the last application, discard the remaining marinade.

Mrs. Harvey Fenton's Lime Wings

20 chicken wings
⅔ cup lime juice
⅓ dry white wine
½ tsp freshly ground pepper
½ tsp rosemary
1 tsp garlic powder

Mix all the ingredients except the chicken wings in a bowl. Add the wings and marinate in the refrigerator overnight. When you're ready to cook, preheat the oven to 375 degrees. These wings are much better when prepared in the oven, rather than on the grill, perhaps because of their delicate flavor. Bake for 10 minutes, then turn and baste with the marinade. Repeat twice, then bake until they're done. These are exceptional—you're going to love them!

Mr. Abernathy's Parmesan Dijon Wings

20 chicken wings
1 stick butter
2 Tbsp Dijon mustard
1 Tbsp garlic powder
2 tsp lemon juice
¼ tsp salt
¼ tsp black pepper
¼ tsp oregano
¼ cup bread crumbs
¼ cup Parmesan cheese

Start out by heating your oven to 375 degrees. Combine the bread crumbs and Parmesan cheese in a mixing bowl. Melt the butter in a separate bowl, then add all the other ingredients (except for the chicken). Dip each wing in the liquid mixture, then roll it in the bowl containing the Parmesan and crumbs. Arrange the wings on a cookie sheet and bake for 25 minutes.

Take them out and turn them once, then return and bake for 15-20 additional minutes until done.

Little Ernie Fratwhiler's Cajun Style Wings

20 chicken wings
1 pkg onion soup mix
1 tsp thyme leaves
½ cup bread crumbs
¼ tsp red pepper
1½ tsp chili powder
1 tsp cumin

In large bowl, combine onion soup mix, bread crumbs, chili powder, cumin, thyme, and pepper. Dip chicken in bread crumb mixture, coating well.

In large skillet, heat ½-inch oil and cook chicken over medium heat, turning once, until done; drain on paper towels. Serve warm and, if desired, with assorted mustards.

Minnie Mae Jensen's Coriander Wings

20 chicken wings
2 Tbsp lemon juice
2 Tbsp brown sugar
1 Tbsp ground coriander
2 cloves garlic, finely chopped
4 Tbsp soy sauce
½ tsp ground ginger
½ tsp cayenne powder
¼ tsp turmeric

Rinse the chicken wings in water, and pat them dry with paper towels. In a small bowl, combine the lemon juice, soy sauce, brown sugar, coriander, garlic, ginger, turmeric, and cayenne. Put the chicken wings in the bowl with the sauce, and let them marinate for a few hours.

Drain the chicken and heat up your grill. When the coals are gray, put the wings on and cook them until they're done. Baste with the marinade a few times in the process. When they're done, discard any remaining marinade and get ready to eat some fantastic wings!

Mrs. Mable Matheson's Garlic Parmesan Wings

20 chicken wings
1 cup freshly grated Parmesan cheese
1 Tbsp (heaping) finely chopped fresh parsley
1 Tbsp minced garlic

1 Tbsp oregano
1 tsp salt
½ tsp black pepper
½ cup butter

Preheat the oven to 375 degrees, and melt the butter in a microwave. While it's warming, mix the cheese, parsley, garlic, oregano, salt, and pepper together in a bowl. Dip each piece of chicken into the butter, then roll in the cheese mixture, coating well. Place the wings on a greased cookie sheet. Bake for 45 minutes, turning at least once in the process. If you're really brave, you can crank up the garlic in this recipe. Uncle Bubba did, once he started preparing it in his restaurant!

Mrs. Oralee Franklin's Texas Tangerine Wings

20 chicken wings
3 tangerines
2 Tbsp honey
2 Tbsp soy sauce
½ tsp ground pepper
2 cloves garlic, finely chopped

Start by peeling the tangerines and squeezing them to get the juice out (you should end up with at least half a cup). Next, grate the colored part of the peel to produce at least a teaspoon. Aunt Irma and her friends would call this the zest, but Uncle Bubba never got that fancy about it. Finally, mix other ingredients in a bowl, add the chicken wings, and make sure they are completely coated. Cover the bowl and place it in the refrigerator overnight.

When you're ready to prepare the wings, preheat your oven to 375 degrees. Remove the wings from the marinade and arrange them on a greased cookie sheet, then bake them for at least 45 minutes or until they're done.

Recipes